Disclaimer

Foul Language Warning: some words may not be suitable to some readers. View at your own discretion.

Trigger Warning: themes of divorce, depression, infertility, miscarriage, new-age feminism, death, murder, mythological creatures, fish, apocalypses, global warming, sci-fy, etc.

Go Save Yourself

Poetry Collection
by *Kate Hodnett*

Go Save Yourself: Poetry Collection

Copyright @2021 by Kate Hodnett. All rights reserved. This book or any portion thereof, including cover art or interior illustrations, text, wording, or otherwise, may not be reproduced or used in any manner whatsoever without the expressed written permission of the copyright owner, excluding in the case of reprints in the context of professional literary reviews.

Cover Design by Tamar Meshki. All rights reserved.

Interior Illustrations by Author Kate Hodnett. All rights reserved.

Editor: Kate Hodnett
Production Manager: Kate Hodnett

ISBN: 9798544488231

This Book is Dedicated:

To Anyone Who's Ever Had Their Heart Broken

I hope you know your worth.

I hope you stop settling for less.

I hope you know that it does, and it can, and it will, get better; as long as you're brave enough to believe that you deserve better.

I hope you stop giving a shit about what other people think that they want for your life. It's yours to live. And I hope you stop sacrificing your own happiness just to keep others happy.

I hope you know that you're stronger than you realize, and that you can re-write your story at any point in time, until you make it to that Happily Ever After, afterall.

*I hope you stop waiting for adventure—
and take that leap—
and above all else--
I hope you know that today, is the day,
to set yourself free.*

Author's Foreward:

To all of you who are afraid to take that leap;

        who are hesitating

        on the edge

        because the unknown appears

        to be scarier- than the known nightmare you're already living in;

This is your sign; do it,

        Go save yourself,

The only thing that is on the

        other side of fear,

is even more love: more

self-love, self-awareness, self-understanding.

There are so many broken people in the world,

and they go around in their brokenness

continuing to break others and

it only breaks themselves even further,

and the cycle just continues and continues,

and all I want to do,

        is just break

            that cycle of brokenness;

I want to make people feel hope again,

              feel whole again

    any way I can, even in the midst of their brokenness,

and I think that, my life experiences, and in particular, my writing of those experiences in brutally honest, raw, and vulnerable ways

    are the main tools I was given to give to others as weapons they can now wield in their own wars of the psyche. Little red strings of promise

tied to a stranger's finger as a reminder,

    to let them know, that none of us are alone in our suffering,

    but together, we can heal more than we ever could on our own.

"I used to think the worst thing in life
was to end up all alone.

It's not.

The worst thing in life is
to end up with people
who make you feel all alone"

-Robin Williams

"The hunger for love

is much more difficult

to remove than the

hunger for bread"

-Mother Theresa

"We are our own dragons
as well as our own heroes,
and we have to rescue
ourselves from ourselves"

-Neil Gaiman

"If Love becomes too painful,
then it's time to let that love go
and save yourself;
You have to keep this in mind
because you'll be able
to find another love,
but not another self"

-Robert Tew

<<the quotes that broke my chains>>
<<now let me help you break yours>>

Part One

the Damsel in Distress

"False Perceptions"

When I first met you
I thought that time stood still

but really the clock
just ran out of batteries,

and that's how we cloak ourselves
in the illusion of magic, isn't it?

"A Love Poem"

There's no one else
I'd rather fall madly and deeply
into the routine of monotony and monogamy
with than you.

"Vows"

Do you solemnly swear to
embrace the feeling
of being undesirable and domesticated
for the rest of your life
as long as you both shall live?

"Promises"

...what good is a future
together, if you treat me
like shit, here in the now?

"Why the Mona Lisa Won't Smile"

The problem with beauty
is that people become immune to it
at a rate of change that is parallel
to a steeply dropping negative slope,
until it flat-lines on the there goes my
eX-axis.

I mean, I understand better than anyone hun,
that staring at the same pair of eyes day in and day out,
must be the 8th circle of hell, not the 8th world wonder;
the last chore on an ever-growing to-do list—
find ways to still be attracted to someone
who you once thought was just that.
Now it's just the same old same, same hair, same skin,
same laugh you've heard a million times
falling now on deaf ears. Things that used to be enchanting
unadulterated magic, fade into the cheap parlor tricks they always
were.

We won't be the first casualty.
Or the last, I assure you.
Don't believe me? Just place the Mona Lisa
at a gas-station bathroom in Mississippi
and see how many people fail to appreciate good art.

"The Love Language of Pigs"

i stand before you to deliver my soliloquy

trying to cover the distance as it

threatens to swallow our marriage whole.

you speak to me from behind your phone again,

mouth moving, but lacking substance.

and this is the way we live.

my green eyes try to lock onto yours if

only for one holy second but

your eyes are locked on the screen again,

and this is the way we connect. your hands on

the phone, the computer mouse, the console controller,

on everything but me.

and this is the way we live.

the first little piggy built his house of straw,

the second in sticks,

but we built ours on false hopes, burnt wicks,

blunt jokes, and whiskey dicks,

and this is the way we love.

"How to Make Good Love Go Bad In Four Steps or Less"

Step One:

"Damn, those grapes
were so ripe and juicy."

"Agreed."

"Can you put the rest
of them in the fridge
so they don't go bad?"

"Sure."

He forgets to put the rest of them
in the fridge. So she does it herself.

Step Two:

"Hey it'd be cool if we
ya know interacted with each other
sometimes"

"Agreed."

"Cool, so like, Friday maybe?"

"Sure."

He forgets to show up on Friday.
She wonders why she has to beg
for the bare minimum
and if you have to beg for love,
is it even worth having?

Step Three:

Repeat stanzas

one and two again

every

week

for the next

52 weeks.

Step Four:

Scratch your head in confusion
and have the gall to wonder out loud
why the grapes have turned into raisins
and why your ex-wife values dialogue over diamonds.

"Fragments"

You look past me, *not at me*—

seeing through me
as easily as I can see
through the bedroom
windows, bare-faced
from the curtains you never
Hung.

You see through me
as easily as I can see
through the empty wine glass
on the counter, waiting
for me to want to wash away
the last of it. You see through me
as easily as I can see through
the hypocrisy staining
the windows at your church,

You see through me

but you don't see me,

when I am there, all of my fragile
Ego laid bare at your feet, putting my
Desires on display like you deserve the right
to be granted free admittance
into the art museum of my mind,
no you still don't see, *me,* putting my heart
in your hands asking you to hold onto it for me
just for one sec while I run to the ladies' room,
only to return, *lost,* when I *find*
out you've misplaced it again; *you don't see me*
opening up and reading every inch
of my body to you *line by line*, I guess you

get bored reading the same book twice, but listen,
if you just stick around long enough to reach the climax
it'll really be worth it in the end I promise and I don't make promises
I can't keep but you,

you do,

and you don't see me

getting tired of keeping up
with all the ways in which
I can't keep
killing myself for someone
*who doesn't even value
my ability to cheat death.*
and I've fought way too hard
to even be here,
breathing, to not be happy while
my heart's still
just barely beat beat beating itself up
over all the ways
in which I can't keep letting myself down
by letting you in. again.
Second chances turning into thirds then fourths then fifths
until I've broken myself down into unrecognizable fragments
of a woman who doesn't know her own worth. For what it's worth,

You don't even see when I have nothing left

to give you. Holes in the soles of my wet socks,
but I'm so comfortable being uncomfortable now
I can't even fathom taking them off. Holes in the soul
that I house, the tenant an obvious flight risk

one more missed payment away from taking off.

"I Can't Do This Anymore"

I'd like to make a deposit please.
One more slip up,
of misplaced trust,
like the time I saved up 400$ to buy you a grill
(because who doesn't love burgers, right?)
and then you let your friend borrow it
(because who doesn't want to love thy Neighbor
as you love yourself, right?)
but then it's returned with rust
because it was left out in the rain overnight.

I wish I could say that was the worst thing
that ever happened to me,
but I think we all know how many
times Caesar got stabbed by those
he trusted most, and I still pick at the
scabs of scars more important
than your imperviousness.

Did I ever tell you bare refrigerators make me
uncomfortable? Where's the pictures?
The art-work? The doctor's appointment reminders?
The coupons? The mustard stain? Why would you want
stainless steel looking back at you empty-handed?

I can't do this anymore.

Pretend the little things don't bother me.

"H2-No"

On really bad days
I don't want to leave
the shower and face the music
of how miserable I've become, so
I beg the tub to fall through the floor--
transform into a submarine and
take me far away from here-- but still,
you find me, pull back the curtain
on my little fantasy escape, and tell me
to stop wasting the water bill.

"There's No Magic Here"

Anywhere I look.

Are you there,
in the secret garden
circle of shrooms?

Are you there,
in the cupboard
in the wardrobe
in the antique clock

how about the broom closet?

Are you there,
Atlantis, in the tub
where I've housed so many
fantasies run dry?

Are you there,
behind the platform
the south wall of bricks
the leaning tower
the cold shower
another hysterical fit?
or maybe there in the bathroom
after another I don't give a shit?

The halls are empty too,
empty here, empty there,

Your emptiness it seems
to have filled the void

everywhere.

"One Eyed Pirate"

The tale is simple
because it's true
a partially blind pirate
sailed the ocean blue;
braving waves and krakens
in search of the gold he HAD
-been dreaming of for decades-
with a patch on his eye and
the wind in his sail,
he weathered the seasons
and searched on despite rain or hail
scouring the water and the land
for anything beautiful
buried in the sand....
Yet all that,
he was trying in vain to find---
because as I said,
the ole hoot
was partially blind
and spent seven eons scouring the sea
for a treasure he had already tossed out
Unknowingly...

"Trust Me"

You sit across from me
at the table, and demand
that I trust you
more (failing to see the irony
that every man who made demands
abused my trust entirely).

The silence between us swells.

You're waiting on me to give
you something that you don't
want to put the time in to earn.
But "I've already earned it" you say,
"you gave me the keys years ago"
Yea, I say, and then you lost them,
and I didn't have a spare made, so
now here we are, both locked
out of the apartment we shared
standing on the steps, going nowhere,
and instead of
taking a moment to find a way
back in or make amends,
you do what they all do,
and make demands.

"Reality-Check"

You're not in love with me--

You're in codependency

& familiarity;

Not in love with me as a person—

but the idea of having another person around—

Not in love with me as a soul—

just more so comfortable

in the situation you already know.

Not bound by love or true commitment

but by the pressures of society & resentment

No worries, though, hun,

I'll stand tall in my contempt,

in the contentment to set us both free.

"Stranded With One Word Responses"

We were never more than forced words
You and I- between gritted teeth and half-assed smiles;
Never more than a carefully rehearsed bare minimum routine
Hello, goodbye, Goodmorning, goodnight
Never more than false promises and slow starts
or heated blood in beaten hearts
Nothing more than Strangers & Distance- whole
Worlds apart while sitting in the same room;
just shadows of our former selves longing to
crawl our way out of the decaying tombs.

"Kids Games"

Unlike the hungry hippos
and monopoly tycoons,
always hungry & putting on the Ritz,
we were naïve little shits
building our house of Jenga Blocks
      the odds against us

             always Stacked
                 higher
                 and
          higher
                 both of us
          always
          pushing
               & pulling
        from all the wrong
               angles
until there's nothing left to do
        but watch it all
            fall
            down

who won?
when we both lose?

"Exotic Fish"

You make me feel like an exotic

Caribbean angel-fish,

hand-picked out of the ocean

and delivered to your door

to be a cherished part

of a prized collection

stowed away in the corner,

like background noise,

just the unnoticed

filtering hums of a

self-sufficient ecosystem

watching the rest of the world

pass by the glass

just another beautiful thing,

proudly showed off,

but loudly overlooked.

"Plenty of Fish in the Sea"

It was perfect when you
were trying to gain my
affections- when you were
trying to reel me in—
It was nice when I was on the hook—
You were good as gold and sweet as sin—
but when I was in the boat
all yours to have and to hold---
you abandoned ship, left me alone, and away
you began to swim, leaving me to
suffocate in the absence
of what could have been.

"The Haunting"

The washing machine rattled furiously,
threatening to spew forth its contents
in a violent exorcism,
Screw this.
I have too many muddy skeletons
of my own hanging in the closet
to be held responsible
for your dirty laundry.

"Closed Eyes & Little White Lies"

It's okay darlin'
Care less
and less,
I see
You're so careless
you might forget how to breathe;

...sometimes I wonder if love is enough
as you say "I love you" and then leave
and as I say "I love you"
and then wonder what that means....

"The Signs"

All I asked for was a sign god-damnit,
God, just one huge neon flashing sign
that I was doing the right thing,
because I'm so obsessed with doing the right
thing I always end up doing the wrong thing;

All I asked was for one sign,
and the universe sent me

3 tornadoes, 2 car wrecks, 1 heart split in half
4 deaths of close friends, 5 plagues,
no wedding dress 3 days before the ceremony,
a car that wouldn't start on the way to rehearsal,
The sacrifice and rebirth of my own soul,
7 toads, 2 turtle-doves, a partridge in a pear tree,
8 fortune cookies saying "get the hell out,"
9 writings in someone else's blood on the wall,
and one painfully accurate gut feeling,

All of which I still chose to ignore
because I don't believe in signs.

"The Bad Thing about Good Guys"

Is that you don't see the heartache;

I swear this one's different Mama; he's clean cut, clean shaven, never curses, doesn't drink, doesn't smoke, doesn't yell or raise his voice in anger, prays over his food, weeds his grandmother's rose garden, hugs his mother, is a really shitty liar, has no desire to cheat, never gambles, isn't reckless with his money. Zero scandals. Zero arrests. Zero tattoos. Never even got a speeding ticket.

I spent a lot of time picking this one, Mama. Checked a lot of boxes to make sure that I wasn't going to make the same mistakes others made. He was nowhere near as rough around the edges as some of the other men around here, right?

I guess that's why I was blindsided when "bad" traits still emerged in someone I had spent 5 years deeming as someone "good" on paper. Traits like:

Selfishness. Self-centeredness. Disconnectedness. Inability to prioritize. Inability to manage time efficiently. Inability to communicate or interact. Ingratitude. Codependency. Insecurity. Immaturity. Disconnected from reality. Inability to be grounded in reality. Inability to be serious, and even lower attention span. Zero intimacy. Zero ambition. Zero goals in life other than father biological offspring. Zero sense of romance. Zero appreciation. Zero admiration. Zero effort. And everything dwindled down to zero. 0. Zero.

And who knew all those tiny cracks and fissures in our foundation would hurt just as bad, as the bad boys who were always more upfront about not being good—they at least never pretended to be something that they weren't; never made false promises.

I don't blame them though. Any of them. I blame myself for such linear thinking; people can't be measured out by teaspoons of good or bad— We are all everything and nothing at the same time, two halves of the same ever-changing whole. No one is ever all one or the other, yet rather, a stirring of both, all at the same time; two odds at ends; the yin and the yang. And love should never be devised by logic alone, a cruel calculation that I derived, a moment too late; logic and love do not co-exist; the very nature of love itself is illogical, which makes it, all the more, a fleeting fantasy. But while we're being logical, the very traits which I grew to hate in him, were the very traits I possessed myself when we first met (insecurity, immaturity, communication issues, codependency, fear, and control), I own up to all of that, and it takes two to tango off the edge of the world,

but my only saving grace was that I grew up and grew out of those behaviors and things which no longer served me gracefully, and as such, I don't even mind being the Bad Guy now.

"All the Little Things"

I'm going to miss all the little things
the most:

your eyes holding mine from across the room
        as if drinking me in was your drink of choice
your fingers running through my hair
the sunshine and your lips both fighting for a spot
        to kiss on my shoulder, in that soft morning afterglow
breakfast in bed, groggy-eyed, grumpy and undeserving
        of love, yet still having it served to me on a silver platter

your hands on my hips as we dance in the kitchen
        to my favorite song
your beard on the nape of my neck
you asking me what I did today in a way that says—
        I know you moved mountains, so tell me which ones
you drawing up a candle-lit bubblebath and
        asking me if there's room for two?

your arms pulling me in close at night
        while your mouth makes sure each freckle is still
        accounted for
your midnight picnics underneath the moon
        when my cravings hit just right,
        leaving us howling in unison
you picking wild tiger lilies and setting them next to
        me on the kitchen counter, commenting on how I too
        am one of nature's beautiful, untamed things

                                [Oh wait, no,
Damn I really let my imagination run wild again, huh?

Because you never did any of those things…

Trying to find things I'm going to miss
is like grasping for straws in a world that's banned straws;

or trying to breathe clean air in a world that gets off on
suffocation, pollution, and white noise

I mean, I guess I'll miss….

the way you made me feel like I was the soul
owner of the world's only invisibility cloak;

and that all I needed to do next
was collect the other two hallows,

to be the master of Death.

"Going Through the Motions"

Iron the pants
Wash the dishes
Water the plants
Plant a kiss on my cat's forehead

Going through the motions

Iron out your attitude
Wash the tears off my face
Feed the dog. Sweep the floors
Put the roast in the oven
Watch you walk out again
Flip you off as you leave

Going through the motions

Mop the bathroom. Smile for the guests
Peel the onion back layer by layer
Scrub all the bullshit off the toilet
Eat dinner with the skeletons in my closet
So I don't have to eat alone again

Going through the motions

Schedule your dentist appointment
Hang your dirty laundry out to dry
Take the trash out on Tuesday
Pack my shit and leave On a Wednesday

Going through the motions

"50/50"

All I really wanted was for you to meet

me halfway, but since that's far too much to ask for

I guess I'll settle for splitting right down the middle;

You can keep the dog, and I'll keep my dignity.

You can take the pity, and I'll take the blame.

You can give me grief, but I'll take the growth.

"Stalling"

Don't I mean anything to you?
Spending the date we designated for
our wedding anniversary
with your friends;
We were nothing more
than the sum of
all the lies
you told yourself about
loving me (rather, the *idea* of me)
all the pretense and pretend
and make-believe
ideas to be read
but if there's no spark to sustain us
then we're both stranded
when the battery runs dead.

"Til Death Do Us Part"

You throw those words out at my feet

like a pair of shackles;

Smirking because, you've got me now right?

"no way out until my pretty little heart

stops beating" huh?

I throw them back at your feet

where they belong;

Smirking while I tell you scathingly, callously

that after living with you,

I'm already dead.

"Why She Left"

The problem

wasn't that she didn't love you,

The solution

was that she needed to love herself more.

"Manifestation Destination"

I want my dream house to have the **WORKS**
like, air conditioning.
and in door plumbing.
and by gawd- harder water pressure.
Oh!! And windows that open!!
And doors that close!!
Ain't that the way it goes??
maybe even if I got everything
I ever wanted, I'd still be wanting more
but who knows?

> Maybe it ain't the destination at all,
> but who you take the journey with…
> Maybe I wanted more than the shell
> of an empty house to come home to;
> Maybe I deserved more, better, than what you could give.
> Maybe I needed more than a roof over my head
> To truly live.

"Nit-picking"

It bothers me how I can cook
the world's best crawfish pie,
but you'd never know that
because you refuse to eat seafood--
and no matter how much I plead,
you just tell me to stop nit-picking;
but you refuse to know a lot about
me, actually, and I guess that's what I
get for marrying a fool instead of a king.

[[Kintsugi]]

My husband bent to throw the
busted ceramic bowl in the garbage;

No! I shouted, in near hysterics,
It still has worth!

It's chipped... he replied...
We can't eat out of it...

Okay, but look! What a nice
fruit or flower bowl it would make!

And that's how I gave new life
to a thing who's purpose was
not destroyed, but merely
Redirected.

"The Disintegration of a Marriage"

PART ONE:

I'm talking to you through the static

but you change the station again.

I think it's odd how good you are at

tuning out the sound of my sadness, and

I envy you in that way. My empathy

always gets in the way.

PART TWO:

You're talking at me

through the veil

that I don't allow

to be lifted.

I think it's odd how good it feels

to look at your tears now,

and know that they don't

hold more weight than my own;

I walk into the kitchen, make some Ramen,

take a shower, go to bed with a clean

conscience and clear eyes.

"Burgundy"

The color so deep,
and encompassing enough that it
glosses over the laced
curtains- shrouding the space,
that was supposed to be
the room of the living,
in death and darkness.

The color so vibrant
and embarrassing enough that it
schemes and screams on its way down
as it mocks the beige boudoir rug
by dripping its scathing
marks, splattered crimson
Rorschach-blots of my insanity,
on what was supposed to
be pure.

The color so rich
and embracing enough that
the chaise it's bathed in,
threatens to swallow me whole,
there in the hallway of
what could have been.

The color so deep
and encumbering enough that it
hollows out the hues of a home,
that has now become a vermillion tomb,
Here, at the address of my
                painfully empty womb.

"Unsolicited Relationship Advice: A Memoir"

"but you'll never find someone who loves you
as much as he does"

> And what makes you say that exactly?
> Because he kisses my cheek in front of you?
> What if I told you that's the only time he kisses me?
> When it's for show, once a year, at Thanksgiving, and the peck feels like he's kissing his great aunt?
> That's love? The greatest love you can imagine?
> Don't try to fix my relationship honey, fix your own imagination; maybe you could even try to imagine what it's like to have a marriage where you aren't sleeping in separate beds, but maybe that's none of my business.

"no one's really happy past
the honeymoon phase, so get used to it"

> well, I mean, we've been dating for a long damn time so I think mathematically we would've exited honeymoon phase a long time ago, but sure, I understand that there's a general sentiment that post new moon is where all good love goes to die, and where all marriages become a hell-hole that no one ever grows the balls to escape from, so they just secretly stick their balls somewhere else where the grass is greener and bite their tongues while biding their time for the rest of their miserable lives,
> but you don't know I know about your side-bitches,
> so I guess I'll keep playing dumb.

"but aren't you at least comfortable?
why would you ever want to rock the boat?"

> Oh girl, why would you ever want to stay in the same boat when you know it's making you sea-sick? For the kids? You're staying for the kids? To show them that they should bottle up all their emotions and throw them out to sea, just to keep a man happy; and that when the resentment washes up to the tide which it always will, they should just plaster on a smile, and say, but watch how well I can avoid confrontation for decades at a time. So many people stay together because they don't want their kids growing up in broken homes, but fail to realize that they are leaving their kids in homes that continue to break them.

"you'll go to hell
because divorce is a sin"

Oh honey, I know, I know it is. Just like it's a sin to hold hands before you're married right, or laugh with your partner versus laughing at them, or do anything together really, other than give sideways glares and bitch about how the dishes need to be done, and dinner needs to be hot and ready by 7, before you both go to sit on separate couches and plan separate vacations. But, honestly, I don't see how hell could be any worse than this hell I'm already living in, so, kind of a risk I'm willing to take at this point. We all have our own versions of hell, mine wouldn't be fire and brimstone (I love the aesthetic of those) mine would be the suburban housewife confined to four walls and a life of serving a man who won't even look at her for five seconds. I wasn't made for subservience, I was made for equality.

"he can change, though, just tough it out and
wait for him to change"

> Oh okay, like you waited years for him to change? How well is that working out for you? Has he changed yet? Have you saved him yet? How could you ever save him when you can't even save yourself? But I get it, no one's perfect, forgive and forget right, over and over and over again, until the red flags start to look black and blue.

"he doesn't cheat on you, is loyal, and didn't leave
you when you were sick; you won't find a better man
than that; so what more could you want?"

> First of all babe, I kind of hate how men get a "get out of jail" free pass from society when their wife falls ill, because "sickness" and health was part of the vows last time I checked; and nevermind how hard it must be on the wife to ya know, almost die, let's all take out our tissues and jack off the husband magna cum laude because he just oh so valiantly didn't stick his dick in someone else while his wife had one foot in the grave, good job. Much valor. Proud of you. And you truly believe I can't do better this? Better than spending every night alone? Better than never having any real conversation? Like sure, you're right, I guess relationships don't get better than this, but I sure as hell don't want to watch myself get worse simply because I never believed that I deserved better, and I sure as hell would rather die trying to be a better version of myself
> than allow myself to die further for fear of failure.

"I Lied, I Don't Want to Lie In The Bed I Made"

In the space between us

piranhas convene, and wait for the blood bath;

wolves converge, and go for the jugular;

vultures descend, smelling the corpse

from a mile away;

flies gather, in holy matrimony.

and I…

I set up camp on the couch instead.

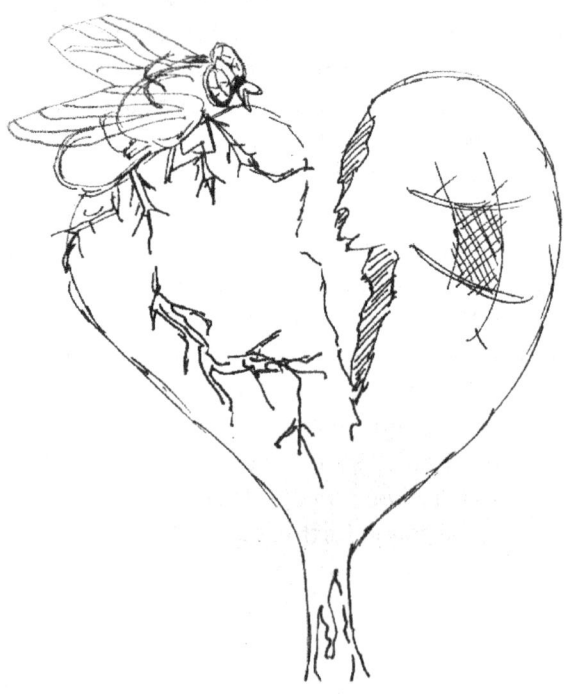

"Where Love Goes When It Dies"

We left pieces of our love,

hidden all over this town,

between the two barstools at the pizzeria,

beneath the ticket booth at the theatre,

down the backroad and round the curve,

following the map that led to

a treasure-trove of secrets--- those

misplaced consolation prizes,

that apparently had an expiration

date before self-imploding;

I tried to go back,

to every nook and cranny

where we used to be,

to recover what we had...

only to find, that this whole time,

there was really no one

ever there at all,

but me.

"unrequited"

I was in love

but

only one of us

was.

"Lost & Never Found"

***"I just lost my love for you
somewhere along the way"***

he says casually,

as if he had misplaced his keys
again; or as if a nickel had fallen out
of his cargo-pockets and buried itself
into the depths of the couch cushions;
as if the fingernail clippers just
grew legs and walked off into the
sunset again,

just that easily,

as if he had accidentally left
his phone on silent and now I had
to call it, pacing around the home
eagerly listening for the slightest reverberation
just so it could be reunited with him again;
as if the crumpled Walmart receipt had somehow
made a daring escape into the oblivion
of his car's floorboard again;

just that easily,

as if the dryer just hellbent on separating socks
from their mates decided to eat one half
of what used to be whole;
as if he couldn't find
his favorite pair of shoes
for the hundredth time, "babe

have you seen my flip-flops?"

he asks, and I know their exact location,
except this time I don't.
I don't know where he left it.
I feel, lost, myself, actually

"how could you lose something so precious?" I ask while my stomach is trying to heave it's way into the wormhole where my heart used to be;

"I don't know,"
he tells me,

"I don't know, isn't good enough"
I tell him,
I tell him I can handle honesty.
I tell him to give it to me straight.
To tell me when/how/why
This happened. He shrugs,

"I just lost my love for you somewhere along the way"

he says casually.

"egregious"

everytime one of the

butterflies in my stomach dies

I write them a

litany

about how my expectations

always turn out to be more exciting

than my

reality

Amaranthine

What good
is a castle
if it crumbles?

How lovely are roses
if they wilt?
Does devastation predate devotion
or is devotion merely a devastation?

Love, I am no princess, and I harbor
no desire for rubies or knights in
shining armor; I only desire nights
where I'm able to disarm my own

shield; unclench my hands
from the sword; and finally,

sleep in beauty
and peace.

The Storms I Weathered Alone

Sometimes when I would fight
for us, I'd ball my hands in fists,
and clench my jaw in resignation
as the rain came down like knuckles
on the drywall; other
times I'd bow my head in prayer
and bring my hands together
in holy matrimony as the gutters
slowly became bogged down with the decay
and debris of leaves who fell too far
too fast; Other times still, I would
cry out over the howling winds, until
my voice cracked, and stand in the middle
of the hurricane I summoned,
wailing out your name,
    and still you'd say "that's nice dear"
        and look the other way.

"Everything You Hate"

everything you hate
about me
someone else will love,

the way I open
cereal boxes like a starving
coyote, hungry, ravenously mad
for all things life has
to offer with no
time to abide by
clear-cut rules or
give a shit about
preserving the sanctity
of the boxes that you
try to stuff me in

or

the way that thunderstorms
whet my appetite in more ways
than one; and the way that I can't
keep my hands to myself—

all of that
ravenousness, will
one day be met with an equal
hunger

and the starvation I endured,
will have been worth it, in the end.

"Questions I Don't Want To Ask Myself
but Always Do"

Will the world end in fire or ice?
Fire, obviously, because all the ice is fucking
melting.

What war has ever truly been "civil" but what's
more,
are we going to have another civil war?
another Brother against Brother
with all this black/white
no gray area, thinking?

Thanks for joining us tonight-
will you be having the

tin-foil hat or broiled lamb?
Democrat Versus Republican?
Popeyes or Chick-Fil-A?
The whole country gone mad
and split right down the middle
like a rabid bitch in heat, covered in fleas,
itching and howling that a country
as great as Rome will never fall.

Are you ever going to get comfortable with Silence?
the explosive way it leaves your head ringing
so that you want to Gogh cut your own ear off

Are you ever going to stop being so comfortable
with Silence?
the sultry way it whispers in your ear
so that you never want it to leave and isolation
becomes your favorite mistress.

Are you ever going to stop "finding yourself"
and actually go and f&%king find yourself

or are you scared of what you'll find

like the little bitch you are, the little bitch you abhor,
who can't stand the heat, yet still itches for more,
howling at the moon as if the sun
won't treat rising one more time
like it's a goddamn chore.

He Loved Me

He loved me passively,

much in the same way
that he would
forget to notice the trees
passing by on the highway miles
when the rubber meets the road;
and even if the entire
forest was on fire,
he still couldn't see the smoke
from the trees

He loved me passively,
in much the same way
that he would play
his handheld videogames
while the ER doctors
drilled another IV into my hand;

He even loved me passively
when I was walking away;
never once,
asking, begging,
crying, or pleading
for me to stay.

"If I'm Always Alone Anyway"

I'd rather be alone
with my freedom

than alone
in your chains.

"They're Just Words"

Floating around in my head

like underwater mines,

just Germanic spiked death-bombs

violent and foreign,

ready to implode at the slightest touch.

Just another big "O"

in my uh-oh SpaghettiOs

Did you spike the punch again, doc?

Just one more punch to the gut

I have to swallow.

They're just. Words. Not your worth.

And maybe one day

I'll love myself

despite what you think about me;

maybe one day I'll stand

with my back to the sun

and not be afraid of my own shadow.

If he doesn't chase you down the driveway
as you leave,
Or fight to show you what it would mean
for you to stay,
You weren't ever supposed to be there,
Anyway.

"The Final Straw"

For me,
I'd say,
Sipping slowly on cabernet,
was when you thought your life,
(your imaginary life,
the one you envisioned
married to a wonderful mother/wife)
was more important than,
my own, actual, life
(like the living, breathing one)
and that I should, be
prepared to die,
(not metaphorically, but literally)
die trying to give you
the "life" you always imagined,
Imagine that?
Because like a child, who just doesn't
understand that life doesn't
always turn out the way we plan;
like a silly little boy with control
issues who can't take no for an answer,
"No, because I want what I want
and I want it now;"
Like a silly little boy who called himself in Love
when really, Love
doesn't look like that;
like turning your back
on someone the moment
things get too rough
or too real
or too many sacrifices are involved
to seal the deal;
The final straw for me,
I'd say was when you
refused to compromise,

on adoption, or surrogacy,
or anything in between
And how my sole identity
and worth lay in the product of me
Laying with you to produce an heir;
And if I couldn't do it,
You could easily find someone who can;
Women were interchangeable;
Little roving pieces
across your chessboard,
you so confident you
could do better
and I was the reason you
were so miserable;

Years down the drain;
Anne Bolyn's head rolls
after the guillotine falls,
at least I still have my
Wits about me, I think.

That, and my freedom,

And my inability to
compromise my sanity
for your vanity,

Was the final straw
in the unraveling hat.

"The Villain"

The day I packed my bags and
moved forward with my life
They looked at me
like I was heartless,

What they didn't realize
though was that I didn't
lose all heart overnight;

I lost it by degrees;
there a little bit more every day
in the silence and absence
of you neglecting me;

And the same people who
never checked on me
while mascara tears ran down
my cheeks, are now the
same people checking up
on me to report back
to you this week.

I remember asking you once,
Why you never kissed me;

Why you only *really* kissed me
Once a year and you said

"if I did it all the time, then it wouldn't be special"

and I remember being appalled that
people could Live like that much
less Love like that;
Reserving the best parts of life for their deaths
Versus devouring them in the here and now
Wholeheartedly;
The kinds of people who acted as
If they had all the time in the world to waste,
When really, we
Had no time left at all.

He told me I needed to lower my expectations;
I said no.
I won't.
But I will go and find someone who can meet them.

"The Phoenix"

You can start over at any time, it's true;
raze your old self to the ground
to raise anew.

Part Two

The Damsel Slays the Dragon

"Mirror, Mirror on the Wall"

I no longer recognize you, at all,

the tired sighs and downcast eyes

the cement wherein your heart lies,

Tell me Mirror, standing tall,

the past, present, and future now recall,

will we ever get back to who we were before?

"No," the mirror falls, and shatters to the floor,

    "you'll become much more."

The Fluidity of Grief

Emotions were never meant for rigidity,

Let them come, Let them go.

You are more than the waves of them,

you are more than what you feel

you don't know.

Don't you Know?

"Abandoned Dreams"

I had to bury everything
that I thought I would be,
out back, behind the shed; I
      shed a tear everytime the
shovel broke the ground
as I lifted the corpse of my dreams
      down down down....
But alas, at last,
from the grave what did rise
springing forth like buds
before my eyes,
but a new set of dreams,
      to my surprise.

"Writer Righting Wrongs"

They see my sad poetry and ask

"who hurt you"

but they never ask
who I've hurt,

and to all the people that I have,

I'm, truly,
sorry.

"Necromancy"

everything she touched
    sprang to life;
flowers bloomed from
    fresh-laid graves
growing in the spaces
    of decay;
hearts that had long
    since stopped-
were beat back to life
    in the same way.

"Why Divorce Makes Me Apprehensive"

I'm not worried about how well I'll adjust

to change; I'll adjust the same way I always do

when life throws me a curveball; I'll hit it straight

on and still bat 1000 on the home-run.

I'm more so worried about how my cat is going to adjust

to change; see, he's been an only child all his life and now

he's going to have not one but two feline roommates and

cats are more ornery and fickle than life itself.

"I Can Open a Jar of Pickles by Myself Now"

The approach has changed--
I have to place the jar on the counter
and really wrangle it with one hand;
sometimes beat it into submission
with a kitchen spoon; sometimes smash
the jar against the floor, and tiptoe
around the glass shards, but I can do it
on my own, and I don't need you as much
as I needed you to believe I did.

"The Monarch"

Once upon a time,
in a kingdom not so far away,
you were an earthworm crawling out of the belly
of the planet, inching your way
towards me.

I was a caterpillar, soft to the touch
and always hungry for something
outside of myself.

Until the seasons changed.

Until I changed.

And suddenly, I had no desire
to rip off my own wings,
just so I could stay on the
ground with you.

Damnit,

You're beautiful.

Don't you know that?

Don't you get that?

Don't you see that?

You don't even have to try---

To be that,

which you already are—

You are beautiful,

Damnit,

Now Start Believing It.

And maybe after

You master the art

Of that, you can actually

Start to believe,

That you're worthy

Of Love too.

"You Shocked?"

I am the taste of electricity,

I am lightning on your tongue,
Sparks on your lips,
Twenty thousand volts,

Running through my
Fingertips.

I Always Seemed To Want More

than men could reasonably give;

attention, time, respect, commitment,

Loyalty,

Love.

And in that space between what I received

and what I lacked, I learned that,

you'd never change

and I was done accepting less than half

of what I'd asked.

"The Dead Things"

As a kid I kept a lot
of dead things close
to me for way too long-
dead leaves preserved in photo albums;
motionless butterflies held captive in amber;
dinosaur bones lining the bookshelves;
books about our dying planet
strewn across the bedroom floor,
the floor that was now lava all
across the world; oyster shells, hermit
crab shells, scallop shells, every vacant pearl-less
shell of a home found a home with me.

Today, I threw them all away.

"New Things"

I'm not the type of person
who is always looking for the next new thing;
In fact I'm the opposite;
I cling to the old things,
old typewriters, old rotary phones,
old books, old friends.

I choose the same meals
from the same menus
at the same restaurants
because I don't want to waste time
trying something new and facing the 50/50 odds
that I might not even like the new thing,
but instead find myself just as hungry and craving the old things.

I made my entire life an ode to the old;
old habits dying hard; old ways of thinking;
old addictions I had no intent on breaking;
old conflicts ripe for the re-making;
old beliefs that kept on replaying.

But then one day I woke up
and I wondered, what if I did a new thing?
And the thought in itself no longer terrified me,
but liberated me.

"My Oldest Pair of Shoes"

I got them in first grade
-light up, with the Velcro-
Together we walked alone
through the halls;
Keep your head down and keep moving;

    You don't need nobody.

I wore them all the way to my high school
graduation (if you're worried about the physics/semantics
of this, don't be, I have tiny feet and they never grew).
The only place we fit in were the corners of the room but that's
where I liked to be; back against the wall, one foot
already out the door; enjoying the solitude of the
Company that came with standing on my own two feet;

one time in art class I even christened them
with the word "Loner" on the bottom sole in Sharpie—
thinking this state of mind would always be
a permanent fixture of my soul, but,

I made the mistake of trading them out
in college for a pair of red high heels;

    I made a lot of mistakes after that.

Now, I finally pull the old sneakers out
from the back of the closet;
They don't light up anymore the way they used to;
and the Velcro doesn't quite stick
but of all the shoes I've ever worn,
the Loner has always been the perfect fit.

"Less Traveled"

				Two roads
			diverged in a wood

One was a hobbled grass pathway
going downhill the entire way
with marble hand railings.
It felt safe. Easy. And the comfort
and security of this path called
my name.

			The other was a path made of
				briar covered stone steps
				ascending in an uphill climb.
			I wasn't sure I had the endurance
		or the strength left to master that route,
	as I was tired of walking the road of life already.

But I knew. Which route the view
would look the best from. And
I knew there's no where else I'd
rather sit in the world than on top,
so I began climbing that painful
ascent, and as such, have yet to stop.

"Disenchanted"

If I can't weave spells over you
let's just call it quits

If skimming through my spellbook
all you see is Latin and not my quips

If leaning over my cauldron all
you see is the mess, not the red lips

bubbling over with giddy gaudy laughter
the lavender smoke rising sinuously to the rafter

If you aren't the equal crafter bearing the eye of the owl,
heart of the lion, soul of a stag, then this ain't what I'm after

If you can't dance with me in the rain unafraid of getting wet,
then let me brew a hex, best we both forget, lest we won't regret;

If you don't see the sparks fly everytime
I hold on high the magic wand
then you're neglecting my inner
Witch of her true power,
shoo frog be gone!

Two Sides of Every Story

I love how you vilified me in yours,

and how they did too, with

their torches and their pitchforks,

pretending that I myself had forked ears

and the devil's tongue; but what none

of them knew so well, was that,

living with you, I already did my time in hell;

and up there upon the pyre,

I've never felt more at Home

than ankle-deep in fire.

"The Bitch Gets Hers"

I've begged groveled
and whined for the last time

Now sit stay and watch me
be wined and dined.

"Don't Forget"

Can't deny I'm a self-sufficient go-getter.
A bitch I was afraid of?
Ain't never met her.
Anything she can do,
I can do better.

"Detonation"

I don't burn my bridges prematurely.
I patiently lace them with
Dynamite
Then wait for you to cross that
Line

self portrait

my mistress's eyes still
sparkle, against all odds,
with their forever-sad ever-green
hues, a washed-out forest where
the last of the fairies play devilish hymns
to drown out all the water under the bridge;
sometimes if you stare long enough
they'll strip themselves bare, down
to nothing but their magic, twisting,
writhing in agony and ecstasy around the iris,
the window to the soul just another blackhole
consuming anything
within range, unapologetically.
I guess all the tears you let loose, mistress,
just add a little extra sparkle and gleam in between the
corner of where your disappointments
make love to your destiny;

there's a little something special, mistress,
in the way the crows' feet
gather at your smile
dropping shiny knick-knacks
as peace offerings
at the head of your breakdowns;
at the gravestone of your buried desires;
at the tomb of your abandoned dreams.

there's something about your cupid's bow lips, mistress
always pulled back at the ready, equipped with quips,
already locked onto their next target;
bullseye precision on a hairpin trigger-happy
trembling kiss that could turn
even the softest hearts to stone
at the slightest touch.

my what blindingly sharp teeth you have mistress,
all the better to grind their bones to dust
with; or at the very least, rip through the sinew of
their heartstrings raw, letting the blood dribble
down your delicate chin. <I'm beginning to think
your mistress is somewhat of a monster, oh she is,
afterall, all the best women are>

there's something about your nose, mistress
that have all the children in the village
convinced you're actually a witch; that and the fact
you live in an isolated cabin in the woods and stand
hunched over a boiling cauldron-- I'm sure has
something to do with it, but the nose is the culprit
surely- that still-small way it points
crookedly, mockingly,
cocking itself in aggressively jarring angles that
make your silhouette slightly haunting; that, or the
way your laugh cackles like embers at a campfire;
or, just quite frankly, maybe it has something to do
with how only you, could make a broomstick
look that good between your legs.

there's no taming your hair, shrew
and I guess the same could be
said of your soul, all shameless, brazen,
and running freely, the tresses fall
down your back in much the same way
that sirens sat on their ship-wrecking rocks, bare
breasted, hair dripping wet with the blood
of all the men foolish enough to stray too far from shore

there's something about the way your
eyebrows arch across your face, not like
gentle rainbows promising peace after a storm, but like
a wanton woman unconfined in the art of free range
orgasms,

creating picturesque
contortions at just the right angles;
the shape of them, so precise and prude, one may
assume you were a nun who only joined the convent
in order to worship the naked man on the cross.

There's something, mistress,
about the way your sun-kissed freckles demand
their own attention on the stage of your otherwise
snow-white
skin, where I can and do get lost in those strange
otherworldly markings,
spending hours connecting all those tiny dots
into un-named constellations that defy time and space.

what I wouldn't do,
what I would do,
to be the reason behind
the dimples playing hide and seek
within your cheeks, that still coy
nature, come out now, come out,
where-ever you are.
The world wishes to gaze upon you
a little longer, mistress,
it's your turn now. You're it.
And what I wouldn't do,
what I would do,
to run wild with your inner child
with you,

just to be there

for the daily spectacle

that is your existence
of grandeur.

"Alone is Not the Same As Lonely"

We live our lives in fear
of loneliness and the unknown,
but in the unknown lies infinite possibilities
just waiting for you to leave your comfort zone;
and in the loneliness lies the better half of
who you could become, if you only took
the time to sit with no one but yourself.

The Dance

The Native Americans did it first
huddled around their campfires,
feathers to the wind,
feet to the earth, arms to the sky,
breathing smoke art into motion,
and transforming death into life;
--- the witches caught on quickly,
with their nude soirees in the woods,
the sorcerceress' transmuting darkness
into magic, into pure unfiltered freedom.
I think it is our turn now,
to rise up on our toes, to dance our way
across the ashes, to leap over the quicksand,
and to leave this life only after the standing
ovation, winded after finally winding down,
the music box ballerina gone rogue,
the world danced into submission.

"It's Not That I Don't Love You"

Sure, I don't want to lose you
but more importantly
I don't want to lose myself
Anymore than
I already have;

"Tarot"

If my life had to be summed up by
a card in the tarot deck,
it would be the tower,
high walls, lightning, hysteria,
death, black cat omens,
chaos as the default.

"Definition"

I no longer wait for you

to tell me

who
I am.

Soon you will find comfort
in leaving your comfort zone.

"The Woman in the Red Dress"

You've been painted a hundred times before, Love, but never like this.

Sure, painted as the Femme-Fatale in every Sherlock Holmes novel, or hell, it even extends to kid's mystery board games now, and still the world doesn't have a Clue. Scarlet doesn't give a shit who did it where, she just wants to go home and read Clarissa on her iPad.

Hun, you've been painted as Rossetti's rosy model, poised with chalice in hand just to coyly commend your chivalrous man; I mean, sure, he got the brush strokes right at least though, as only men can do, giving credit where credit is due.

There you are again, in Munch's "Dance of Life" the symbol of passion- just as stoic as ever. I'm sure your partner is insinuating superficial innuendos like how delicious the oyster hors d'oeuvre were, then he'll place one hand up your back and ask you to smile for him, like you're a ventriloquist's dummy.

You're there in the film "Pretty Woman" which is basically the only thing you could ever be, apparently. As if it were ever that black and white, or rather, RED. As if that's supposed to be flattering. Damn, Jessica Rabbit your brains sure do look good in that outfit. History in the making. If you want to know how Marilyn seduced Kennedy, just ask the red dress.

And here I am, lips to yours, having to breathe back the humanity into your lifeless sex symbol corpse on the corner of the Spring Break beach-house resort, praying you'll have it in you to cough up all the bullshit. Even if you were Neptune's daughter, hun, you don't actually have to swallow the sea water.

You are neither virginal sacrifice nor textbook succubus, but rather, both simultaneously—they're two sides of the same coin, that very quarter that you used to play "Summer Wine" on the Jukebox that one night in Anaheim.

You are neither the red-breasted black widow nor the empty chested blood-drained fly, but rather, you are the intricate web woven between their convoluted waltz.

Some would simply say your head's hung low in longing and desire; but they fail to immortalize your shame, your regret, your loneliness, when there's nothing left of you as soon as you take off that dress. Nothing more than an exotic chameleon shedding her skin, bones held together by small red ribbons, threads laid bare.

Shoes, matches, imported wine--- things that belong in a box. Women, however, do not.

Let me paint you in a new light baby, wiping Cheetoh crumbs on your sweatpants. Don't sweat it, Love, you'll be free soon, all fabric unravels eventually.

The Witch in the Woods

I don't think she's ever needed
anyone
and I think that's
exactly
what makes her so
terrifying.

"I Don't Think I Believe
In Love Anymore"

Not in the way I used to cling to
the idea of it, that first draft
scribbled on paper, the final draft
polished and refined, waiting,
to be heard, to be felt

Not in the way I used to-- wish
upon a star, now I just watch the
stars burn out. I'm still afraid of
the dark, but, I've learned to sit
with my fear as if it were my only friend

I don't think people are capable
anymore of putting their phones down
at the dinner table or wanting to wake up
and appreciate the warm body next to them versus
immediately lose themselves in those cold black
screens.

I don't think we want to connect.
Past the superficial.
I don't think we can.
I always drown in shallow water,
Give me your muddy puddle and I'll lie in it face up
bloated and blue. But give me the ocean. And I'll make
pearls out of my pessimism. I'll make tsunamis swell
until they crash through that wall hiding the human
heart. Its behind it, right? Just beyond the horizon line?

I just don't think I believe in you
anymore, I just don't think I need
a hero when I am so busy believing
I can rescue myself.

3 Blind Men

I approached the first one
and asked,
    "I am a parcel of truth, will you accept?"

        He replied that he preferred to live a lie.

I approached the second and
 said, "I am a treasure, beyond all measure, the likes of
which others can scarcely compare, but you will have to
dive to the bottom of the ocean to recover me?"

      He replied, "that's too deep, and I cannot swim."

I approached the third
and laughed, I set loose my soul
upon the earth, and in my wanton wrath
      said "all that I have
      is yours to have"

      and he replied, "it's too much, take it back."

Apologies

If you're going to apologize
    you better find a word better
    than "sorry" this time;
Better sail to the Bermuda Triangle,
    and get lost trying to
    dig up a new old term
from the forgotten city of Atlantis;
    don't come back until
    you can find that one,
    word,
Something with strength,   Conviction,   A redemption
arc, something that invites both   fear and   hope,
panic   and   peace;   destruction
and   rebirth;   the ancient and the new;
    the end and the beginning;

    Something like

    "Apocalypto"

    Or--
    "My world would be lost"
    Without you

    Or "I'll never put you through
    another devastating catastrophe
    again."

Or maybe, for once, you could bring back something
that was less reminiscent of the disastrous fantasy
we found ourselves living in;
and deliver something more along the lines of the
actual truth; maybe I deserved to have that premonition
revealed, regardless of how cataclysmic the disclosure.
Maybe that would have been better than your empty

apo (l) og (ies) that could not deliver
my deliverance.

                    Maybe Apocalypto
                     wasn't a promise
                  to never end, at all,
          yet rather a salvation found only
             in the beginning of the end,

                          afterall;

        maybe it meant something like,

                     "even the
          greatest of civilizations fall,
                    and our expectations
                  were no exception"

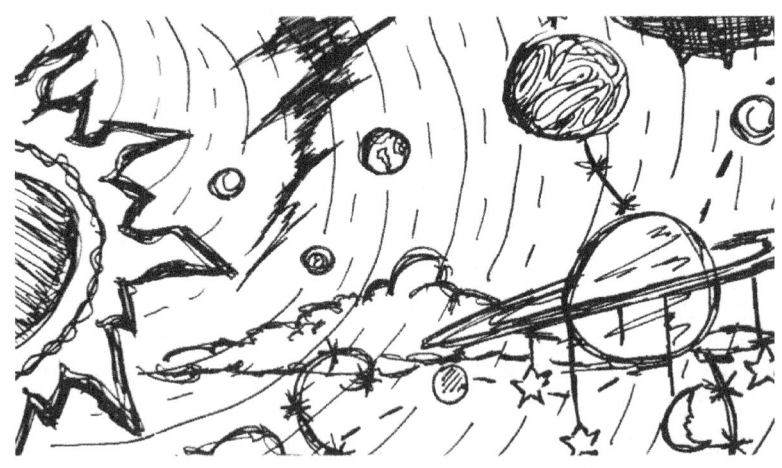

Moving Forward

Why spend time crying
      over the last chapter
when you could spend time writing
      the next, even better One.

Based on "Wild Geese" by Hera Lindsay Bird, inspired by Mary Oliver's original "Wild Geese"

■■

"Wild Goose Chase: Self-Indulgence Edition"

You do not have to be good.

                                  I'm sure there are people out there
doing worse things
than what you're about to do, right?

Right or wrong—
Poetry, I mean Love, can only ever be right, or am I wrong?

                    Meanwhile, the man armed with his affairs—
crushes his wife's wind-pipe
Meanwhile, the father smothers the wide-eyed toddler not
with love but with her favorite blanket
Meanwhile, God lets their bodies rest in pieces at the bottom
of a chemical vat
Meanwhile, the women flock like geese to the jail to offer
their ovaries to the killer's seed
Meanwhile, God doesn't look surprised when Adam still has
the apple stuck in his throat
Meanwhile, Bonnie takes just as many bullets
to the chest as Clyde
Meanwhile, God paints his sunsets with just the right shade
of bloodbath
Meanwhile, Ophelia doesn't feel like calling another man
"daddy" right now

Meanwhile, God-damnit, what's good for the goose isn't
always what's good for the gander!

                        Meanwhile, in times of doubt, I ask myself
what would Lilith do?

Meanwhile, you don't have to beat yourself up over not
being someone's punching bag
Meanwhile, I start fights because my favorite disposition to
have sex in is anger
Meanwhile, in an alternate universe maybe I'm doing a lot of
things differently, or, at the very least, doing you.
Meanwhile, you're too focused on nature imitating art to
appreciate the urgency here
Meanwhile, I slip into something a little more comfortable,
like a straight-jacket
Meanwhile, Persephone seduced Hades just to find out death
is nothing but nothingness.

Tell me about your despair, yours, and I will tell you mine.

You don't even have to be good
at anything if it all means nothing,

which may be kind of liberating--
You don't even have to be good
at poetry, anyone can do it—

Just regurgitate all your putrid secrets
into mouths eager for humiliation
and desecration— like
Wild geese--- standing where you shit
or shitting where you stand,
all of the shit you stand for
is bullshit anyway
when all you do is fly south

at the first sign
of discomfort.

Why can't you sit in it?
Tough it out?
You really think it's natural to live--

(Much less love)
On the run?
No, you don't *have* to be good at
Jumping the gun
but it never stopped you from
firing one
straight into that unnatural V
in the sky,
blow the load and let die
and I'm supposed to think
the lack of commitment
is romantic?
I mean in a while, you'll love me tomorrow.
Meanwhile, tomorrow never comes.
Tell me your despair,
yours,
and I will tell you

that my Desires,
        I mean despairs,

                never did fly

        I mean fall, in

    line.
Meanwhile,

Duck duck goose,
All you gotta do is let loose, sis.
you don't even have to be good.
And yet here you are, being good
at the only thing
you don't even have to be good at---
being good.

"They Say"

Imitation is the highest form of flattery,
But quite frankly, I'm just offended;
Two weeks in and you've already committed
the one unforgivable sin;

replaced me as if I'm easily replaceable;

I mean sure her Double D's
have more weight than her brains, and sure she
has 4 kids already so at least we
know she's fertile right-- your one requirement
for a worthwhile woman-- now fulfilled; and I mean sure,
she already broke your heart 3 times in 2012 back
when she blew some guys for blow,
after blow, after blow, behind your back,
but I get it, you two have history
Together, and now, a future, too, isn't that a fact? that's
fantastic, and maybe at this point, just maybe, I'm not
even being sarcastic? And maybe my favorite part is
how she dyed her hair red for you,
I mean I must say the resemblance is uncanny darling,
Do you want me to hand her my pearl necklace too?
Would that do it for you? Your very own makeshift
Aphrodite rising from an artificial sea, tell me my
darling, How does it taste-- the knockoff version of me?

"Why Yes, I Am the Crazy hEx"

Milk of the almond
Wart of the toad
Two shades of somber
As we brew the first load

Eyes of the fox
Skin soft as virtue
Wit sharp as indigo
Enter karma, on cue

Dragons breath hair
A little more, To the right,
Pulled back with a sneer;
The sirens delight.

Your gift of rejection became
my mantra of empowerment.

"They Called That Love"

When I was 5 a boy pushed me down in the sandbox
and they called that Love.
The funny part is that I was the Queen of the Sandbox
and I enjoyed eating dirt.

When I was 10 I had an unrequited crush on this boy
with blue eyes, and I called that Love.
The funny part is that I believed love could only
ever exist in half-measures, or parts that would never be
whole.

When I was 15 my body, which for so long had been
ridiculed, now became a commodity but
Not my mind, and they called that Love,
And I thought it was funny how someone could only ever be
attracted to the most boring part of my physical existence.

When I was 20, he expected me to live off of crumbs
Without starving and they called that Love,
The funny part was that I thought it was more
Than enough at the time.

When I was 25, he made promises he just couldn't keep
And they called that love,
The funny part was that I've always found that lies
were easier to believe, easier to swallow, than the truth.

When I was 30 I finally found the strength
To say no, I will not continue to settle for less than
what I'm worth, and for the first time in my life,
I called that
Love.

Reciprocity

I will no longer give myself away, you see,
to those who are incapable
of giving me the same- court-e-sy.

Boredom

To be frank, I'm just
incredibly bored
with people who fail
to recognize
my worth anymore

"No Collars for Callers"

Ladies, listen closely.
I'll teach you how to channel your inner Medusa.
Like a snake shedding its skin—
here's how you lose what no longer serves you
and switch into a resounding Resiliency.

There's nothing wrong with powdering
the truth up a little
if you don't like what you see in the mirror.
Maybe a little low-dim light, and a fifth of whiskey is
all I need to make my ambitions look better, after-all.

Maybe I shouldn't have worn that shade of lipstick…

I used to feel guilt like a gun-powder punch to the gut,
but now it's as subtle as smushing an ant
underneath my liberating red-lined Louboutin.

I've survived trainwrecks without pain killers,
so if you think the brass-knuckled lamp on the boudoir
intimidates me, then you're wrong---

Trading morphine for more of the pen.
Blocking it out with ink blots
in the shape of yet another silly syllogism
(All dogs like to beg. All men like to beg.
Therefore all men are dogs, and I beg you to differ)

----but that's just the Adderall talking I'm sure,
 just another amphetamine driven enthymeme---
like the belief that "oh she wears a choker around her neck,
so she must enjoy being somebody's bitch."

And every time you have an itch you need to scratch,
you always call me, but honey, it ain't my fault

you're riddled with fleas.
No more riddles, please!
(you'll exclaim when you've had enough of my caustic tongue),
Can't you be more debutante?!
(you'll demand when I turn out to be more than what you want).

I'll never wear a muzzle honey,
it just doesn't bring out my eyes.
You may be all bark and no bite,
but that's not the way I write
or the way I writhe,
much less thrive
on the rinds you
left behind.

Cause the shit you left in my yard,
see it started to smell.
You expected me to bag the shit up,
but you never anticipated how widely it'd sell.

"Making the Arrangements

for Estrangement"

The strangest part of loving you

was that unexpectedly

underneath all the blindly dizzying

rush of rejection that kept me entwined; was that

I really learned how to love, all the parts of me

you left behind.

The strangest part of losing you

was that unexpectedly

underneath all those pieces

of you I just couldn't find; I was able to

find the pieces of myself, that

had long since been lost, forgotten,

and undermined.

"What do you want out of life?"

I want to be able to tell Allen Ginsberg
that my good-looks did in fact,
buy my groceries.

I want to be able to tell Maya Angelou
that the bird is no longer caged, and it
does in fact sing louder
the higher it soars; I want to be able
to thank her for teaching me to walk
like I have diamonds at the meeting
of my thighs; and how many times
I used that worth to walk right into
living my best, most brazen, most courageous life.

I want to be able to tell Robert Frost,
that I took the road less traveled, and that
it was worth it every lonely step of the way,
because even at the end, when I found Nothing other
than Myself, that was somehow, Everything.

I want to be able to share a pint with Bukowski
In the middle of hell with the hounds barking,
Where we could in agony, already endured,
Ask the devil if that was all he got? And to
Pour us another round, as we
Laughed and cried over the ones that got away,
poems, not lovers, memoirs, not memories.

I want to be able to tell Poe that I did in fact
Love with a Love more than Love; that I set
all of my imprisoned passions free, and that I allowed
my heart to ache and bleed and creak
unapologetically underneath the
floorboards of the very earth,
until the day I died, only to be
buried with no regrets.

I want to be able to tell Dickinson
that I was Nobody, too. And that my
Heart never did, quite forget him,
Even after all these lifetimes.

I want to be able to tell Shakespeare that
I made the world my stage, and I played the roles of
poets, paupers, preachers, and mad kings;
But that in the end, my favorite role of all, was simply to just
Be.

I want to be able to tell Chuck Palahnuik,
that I burned all my possessions and that the things
I owned no longer owned me; that the sound the
match made when I struck freedom will forever
be my favorite sound, and how I want to
continue spending the rest of my life
burning failed infrastructure down.

I want to be able to tell Charlotte Bronte

that whatever our souls were made of,
His and Mine, were the same. And that
When I met him, I would know that he
was a man not only worth dying for,
but finally worth writing about.

I want to take back the power that was
stripped from me. Medusa with her head
of snakes, and the headless stone men around her.
I want to cause the sea to foam at the mouth
every time I walk by; or to cause volcanoes to run hot
with lava down the sides; I want to look up
at the stars and cause Orion to loosen his belt;
or give Zeus a reason to confront Hera's jealous rage.

I want to ride the Streetcar named Desire
all the way into Dante's Inferno;
and dab Jitterbug Perfume on my wrists;
I want to carry Water for Elephants,
and wear my Scarlet Letter proudly,
I want to laugh with mirth, and cry with desperation,
and feel the depths of it all, everything in between;
But most of all, I want my greatest achievement
to be, that I was quite simply, unafraid to be me,
unapologetically, and rewrite my story
from one of tragedy to victory

"Queen's Reprise"

Every battle I've ever fought
I've had to fight on my own,
but still I have conquered kingdoms
even while bound to your throne

"Independent"

You were so busy
trying to get me to not
need you, that you failed
to realize that
I never did.

"The Fall"

You fell out of love.
I fell apart.

"Baptism"

I used to bite my tongue until it bled,
The damn thing was just so sharp,
I shouldn't let it loose, you said;

Now I've made a weapon out of all
the words you made me water down
or swallow, so hear them, in your heart
so hollow,

Let them make you anew.
Oh, but I forget, there's nothing
you hate more, than confronting
the truth.

The Raven

collected enough Stones to line
velveteen pockets with a heavy finality;
spoke with such repetitious conviction
that
you couldn't help but listen
to the goosebumps on your skin,
but, the scariest part,
the chapter of the story Poe forgot
to tell about the feathered beast from
hell,
was that the biggest monstrosity of all
was that
She had spent so long
being someone else's caged bird,
Spent so long clipping her own wings,
That when she finally decided that she
was capable
Of flying, she would no longer sacrifice
that freedom
For anyone, or anything.

To my future self,

I hope that you never settle for less
than what you're worth again,

that you
never tolerate or shoulder the injustices
of others

That you can look back on your lost love
and be grateful that you found the most
Important person of all, yourself.

I hope that you look in the mirror
more often, your reflection deserves
your attention and your forgiveness,

I hope that you leave the past behind entirely.

I hope that you never hesitate again,
that you kiss unabashedly
that you converse unapologetically,
that you live courageously,
and love as if you've never been let down,
and,

I hope that you start to believe in yourself, again
as much as you believe in others.

To all the people standing on the edge,
but are hesitant to take that leap,
I hope you never become so fearful of
change that you allow yourself the grave
injustice of staying the same.

"I Will No Longer Dance"

Around Men's fragile egos, entertain
their lies, or take part in the performance
of their half-hearted truths,
nor will I invite myself to be used
by sitting at tables where I always only feel
half-fed and forever starving for more;
Instead, I will confront their demons
head-on and leave their pride
blackened, bruised, and sore.

"Coming Home"

I used to be the kind of person
who envied people who
were comfortable in their own
skin; as I was constantly trying to claw
my way out of my own; but now
I dance the moon into a frenzy,
and bend willows to my will;
Now, the devil runs scared
when he sees my fire,
too intimidated to seal the deal;
Now, the witch defiantly lights a cigarette
off of her own pyre with no intent to conceal
her mystery and debauchery and infamy;
Now where lovers turn to stone
in their complacency;
Now where I create chrysanthemums
out of the rubble and debris of their infirmary;
here where I command the water
in the skies to wash us clean on cue;
Now where wolves howl in their indigo hues,
calling calling calling back to me;
It turns out that here in the house
of my own soul now, surely,
is the most important place
I've ever had the pleasure to be.

A Love Letter

I think it's a damn shame that
we don't write more love letters to ourselves,
so here, I'll take the plunge
and expunge myself--

    Kate,
You are a resilient
fearless flame of a woman
that life has tried countless times
to douse, and still, you re-ignite.
    Kate,
I think your flame is quite
catching if I'm being honest,
not just charming, but devastatingly
catching, raging, devouring
everything it touches and giving
others permission to Burn too.
    Kate,
I like how you're not afraid
of Hell because you're too busy
trying to create Heaven on Earth
out of all the ashes you've already been dealt.
    Kate,
I admire the way you're not
waiting for me to tell you want you want
to hear, because you're so busy not needing
anyone or anything, other than all of you,
that I've never seen a more completely
incomplete thing in all my life.
    Kate,
I love you. I'm sorry I haven't told
you sooner, I'm sorry you sifted through
so much unrequited love you began
to think that you were actually unlovable,
but thank you, for waiting for me, to get

my act together, and I promise this
final act, will be the most courageous yet.
    Kate,
I can't get over how radiant you are.
And how honest you are in that radiance,
how you don't try to paint yourself
as the sun on a rainy day, but rather,
the sun when it's blinding your eyes
while you're driving down the highway
and the stupid car visors won't do shit,
I think it's noble how you assault us all
like that, but how we like
to be assaulted by a broad
so possessing.
    Kate,
what I'm trying to say is that you're
too bright to take in sometimes,
and that, that's okay, the world doesn't
have to stare at you, in order for you
to be seen. So keep shining. Keep burning.
    Kate,
I've waited my whole life to find you.
And now that you're here, I will never
let you go, do you understand? It's not you and
me against the world, it's you and me
re-creating the world.
    Kate,
I know that's no easy task, but I know if anyone's
up for the challenge, it's your crazy ass.
    Kate,
I know I can't bind you, I know you are wild and
free by birthright, but I'm glad I get to know you,
to hold you, to laugh as you attempt to tame small
pieces of yourself
and offer them up on a silver platter to the world,
I think your vulnerability is your strength and for that,
I will always, not so secretly admire you.

Kate,
I love how you loving yourself will
never be enough for you. How you need
others to love themselves too. How fear will
threaten to keep them all trapped, and how you
will want to hand them the key and grin...
while you say, now it's your turn.
So don't keep me waiting, again.

All of my Love,

Take care of yourself,
In whatever form that may take,
Kate

"All That I Needed"

Sometimes
all a man could really give
me was the inspiration for a few
good poems,
and sometimes
that was more than enough.

There are no right or wrongs
Technically
It's all just experiences
and lessons and growth anyway
So even when wrongs end
up being right,
There's not really much left to fear is there?

Anteric

He taught me what healthy love was not,
and how to make my own decisions
without apology and with precision.

Bravura

You're stronger than you know
Although the road has been misleading
        You fear you're all alone
          and your heart will stop it's beating
                My darling, you're braver than the rest
                      Even when you're blind
Don't mind the pounding in your chest
I know that you'll be fine
        The Night has slipped into your mind
          And swirls about in shades of gray
                It eats your thoughts line by line
                  as you pray for God to come with Day
Stand up tall. Be very bold,
Pick up your arrows, lay down your fear
        To fight the Dark; to fight the Cold
        You'll lay your foes to rest right here
                Your bravery comes at a price
            And it makes you have to sacrifice
To save the world you have to die.
But it's okay they won't cry long.
        They knew exactly what you had to do
        And they'll write of your valor in glorious songs
                They're alive because of you
            Although the road is obscure and dark
It's for the world that you must go
So go with boldness in your heart
        My dear, you're stronger than you know.

A Piece for the Critics on Feminism

Sure, some of my poetry may come off as "man-hating" but that's not the intent nor the reality; sure I experience a lot of strong emotions that I like to pen down, but ultimately, even going through periods of disappointment, I realize that we teach others how to treat us, **and we can expect to get that which we accept**. I recognize that a lot of my own hostility towards men was my own unprocessed issues at the time, and my own projections/fears/insecurities that were not rooted in truth or the new version of reality I wished to live in. There is more goodness than we could possibly fathom or imagine, we just have to be brave enough to pursue it; and determined enough to undo- our own negative thoughts/patterns/behaviors like those "toxic man-distrusting" personnas. We can strike a balance, where feminism means equality and peace, not, more pain or isolation or tipping the scales in the opposite direction.

She Was Beautiful

She was beautiful
but not in ways I've seen before; in
the way that she was fierce enough to walk across fire
without wincing,
and capture lightning in bottles
while dancing;
She was delicate enough to land in your life,
and drastically change it with subtle kindness
vulnerability, laughter;
The way she wore her scars like jewels,
adorned with wisdom, experience, expertise;
The way she held her head just a little higher
when she should've felt lower; the way she
Kept moving forward, fearlessly, authentically,
starvingly ravingly mad, to create
A better life.

Bible Belt Beauty

Oh yes, pray for me,
The woman unconfined;
has at last, crawled her
way out of the yellow wallpaper, indeed,

"What Are You Up To These Days?"

I dry and press flowers

in the pages of Shakepeare's poetry;

and I remind myself

that wilted things

can still retain their beauty

even after all these years

You Have to Let it Go,
If You want to Grow

Unclench your fist,
Let the tears flow,
Write down all the
Offenses on a piece
Of paper that you burn
And loose the ashes
To the wind; do it however
You have to, but you have to,
Let it go.

From a Girl Once Afraid of Confrontation

We should always feel confident enough
To say whatever it is we need to say
To not let things build up in falsehoods,
Confrontation does not reduce connection,
Yet rather enhances understanding, and allows
Us to give each other and others better what
They need. It is a liberating freedom to understand
That disagreements or differences aren't anything
To be ashamed of, but are natural parts of the ebbs
And flows of real, authentic, interaction and individual
Growth; Human emotions are fickle creatures; they wax
And wane due to a variety of factors, rainy days, returned
Postcards, spilled milk; but our souls, hum the same
Ever ceasing tune day in and day out; the souls are the thread
Upon which all emotions dance and there are no bad
Emotions; or negative ones; they are all just experiences,
And equally valid parts of life.

how I just don't give a shit anymore about what people think of me:

when I almost died I realized how f&%king silly it was; to live my life through other people's opinions/expectations/wants/needs/viewpoints.... it wasn't their life to live; it was mine, and I had wasted it worried about everyone but myself. They're not the ones who have to sit in misery, or live with my decisions; I was the one who had to live with that, so I didn't want to do that anymore. Also, I learned quite quickly that even the beds I made myself, I didn't have to lie in indefinitely. I could set myself free unapologetically. F&%k, look at Goldilocks, she slept in all the f&%king beds and gave zero shits. And that my dears, is Freedom.

how I stay pretty much happy internally, despite everything externally:

I truly believe there are beautiful moments in every day, even the worst days. I truly believe there is magic if you know where to look; and blessings if you're brave enough to count them before counting your tragedies. Simplicity for me is the key to happiness, and it doesn't take much for me to achieve the desired effect; petting a cat, seeing a sunset, eating macaroni, other cheesy ass shit; I'm super f&%king low maintenance. Always have been. I think because my life as a whole has been so rough, that like, I learned pretty early on that happiness is an intrinsic thing, and that I cannot go through life allowing my external circumstances to dictate my mood. Or else, I always would have found one excuse or the other to not be happy. And to me, it feels truer to who I am at the core, to live in joy and bliss and hope, than to give pain and suffering the reins. My favorite flower is the sunflower.... it's a lot sturdier than other flower species; it can grow in more harsh environments easily; and it grows a lot more than other flowers-- like they can grow over 20 feet tall sometimes, the giant ones... but the main reason I love sunflowers the most (aside from their bright and happy coloration) is that, they always deliberately keep their faces turned toward the sun; no matter what way the sun is facing; and I love that. I also realized that most people spend their lives avoiding pain.... pain is unavoidable, the more you start facing it head on versus resisting it, the easier it becomes to stomach.

how I overcame the fear of the unknown:

sure, it is terrifying not to know what the future holds... but none of us truly know anyway to begin with; and there's also an excitement to not knowing; to having a clean slate; to being able to create or re-create anew. The part of me that clings to predictability and routine for comfort is mortified yes, but I also realize that comfort and stability are only ever temporary illusions anyway, that can be shattered by anything at any time (such as ya know an unprecedented pandemic). Also, as much as I desire calm and predictable and routine, the part of me that longs to live life as one ongoing adventure, doesn't mind the challenges that pop up in that said adventure, and navigating how to be free and to find new ways to incorporate more freedom and expansion into my everyday routine, I'm more so eager and grateful to be given the opportunity to not limit myself, and like I said, my brain really gets off on solving challenges. Now, I'm not going to lie to you. It's not easy. At all. Everyday I struggle with waves of panic and fear and pain and just, a desire to crawl back into my old skin.... to cling to comforts like "a house in the burbs, a lifetime supply of new cars, the security of having someone, a warm body, to come home to everyday even if the love wasn't real-- at least it was consistent and accessible and felt safe; even if it was very mismatched and misguided, at least I wasn't alone" I miss those comforts. But I try to remind myself that my peace of mind and sanity and happiness and health and self-worth are worth more than material things and that I as a person am worth more than the way I was being treated in the context of that marriage and it's relational toxicity. It was preventing more than my growth, but also my prosperity, not just emotional or spiritual but physical. And it's important that we don't idealize our memories of our relationships, but to view them through the realistic lens. All of that fear is there. I choose to feel it, honor it, acknowledge it, process it, but I also am trying to live by the motto "feel the fear, but do it anyway." Feel the (rightful) fear that accompanies jumping blindly off a cliff, but do it anyway. Feel the fear before an interview, do it anyway. Feel the fear of making changes, make them anyway. Feel the fear of rejection, put myself out there anyway. Feel the fear of being alone, be alone anyway.

how I overcame my fear of change:

my fear of change, at the core of it, was nothing more than my fear of losing control... I like to feel in control at all times, of everything. Change is the opposite of control. It is things beyond our control. It is maddening and disheartening and incredibly painful... but it is also, incredibly transformational... and it is also the antidote to stagnation. I no longer had a choice there at the end; I knew beyond a shadow of a doubt that continued stagnation would be the literal death of me. Change became the lesser of two evils. I am human though, and I am not immune to worry or bouts of misery. But most of the time misery is born of, not fully being present in the present moment, so I try to work really hard on grounding myself in the present, and not focusing too much on the past or future. Easier said than done. "to choose being uncomfortable over quick and easy comfort is to confront yourself and your own limitations, in order to push past them" thus, the measure of being limitless is to throw yourself headfirst into the wall of your own limits.

how I'm surviving a divorce without a massive breakdown, either mentally or in the moral fibre of my character, arguably:

All losses are superficial to some degree; like sure, I miss certain things about certain people, certain moments, certain memories, certain ways I thought I saw my future, certain personality traits, but, on a soul level my body/heart/mind often feels better/lighter when I remove myself from certain people or situations that were no longer for my highest good. And I generally try to stay classy about things, she says, while publishing a very deep, invasive, personal poetry book. Shrugs.

"There is Medicine in Your Shadow"

The gypsy woman said to me,
as if having the courage
to go into the deepest parts
of my pain would be easy,
or worth it,
as if moving through the pain
to get to the healing
was easy,
or worth it,
as if knowing that it has
to get worse before it gets better,
makes the worse part any better-
as if spending time with the
darkest parts of myself
was easy,
or worth it

But it was.

It was the most
worthwhile thing I've ever done.
and I'm here
to tell you,
there is medicine
in your shadow, and you're healing's
only just begun.

Yeah, Sis

You might be in love

but that doesn't mean

it's a healthy relationship

There Are Always
Two Sides of Myself At War

My anxiety

versus

my desire

to create a new reality

The Beauty in Grief

After decades of always holding
It together, emotions preserved in cement;
the mirrors in my irises shattered---
my palms opened up like an atomic bomb
my heart was a gateway to the heavens,
       And I wept.

No More Waiting

Watch now,

how I Stopped

Watching
the Stop-Watch;

Wait now,

as I go forth,

and Watch
how I won't

be Stopped.

Once Upon A Candid Conversation With A Friend:

But what if none of us, in general, ever really knows anything? What if we all have just been walking around deaf, dumb, and blind to obvious things right in front of us? What would we do as a collective with that sort of disassociated lack of awareness, or, lack of understanding, or lack of direct communication?

I also think it's a universal human longing really to encounter real emotions in general; to experience the full depth of them; the passion, the understanding, connections that can't be forced or faked or whittered away by time, distance, or offense.

When I was married myself, I had kind of felt, a large part of myself die, which sounds overdramatic but in all serious a lot of my own spark for life and existence was extinguished being confined in a less than healthy dynamic; and, what I ended up fighting for in the end, was not to save my marriage, but to save myself, to fight for myself, to fight to give myself a chance at really living life again and encountering all those emotions that I had repressed or neglected for so long.

I think we all always worry about the next step in anything in life, but the irony is that, no matter how well we plan or pace or time our steps, do we ever really get to choose the path? Or pick the mountain to climb? Or is it all already predetermined for us? Does stepping in certain rhythms give us the illusion that we are in control? And that anything that threatens that false sense of control in our well constructed lives is perceived more as a threat than a blessing?

But just be careful not to take so much pity on the broken things of this world, or to garner too much of a hero complex; because in the end, that disempowers people; and in the end, I think people are far more capable of transmuting their own pain into power than they themselves realize.

Don't we all always keep our thoughts under lock and key and keep our emotions on a tight leash. So then, do we truly have emotions our soul longs to experience? Only to deny our soul of that experience? Out of what really? Fear, honor, commitment, justice, trauma-loops? Who knows, I guess the answer varies for everyone, but I threw away my own key, and now am free to let my mind, or my steps, wander, wherever they may please, and that sort of freedom, is so liberating; especially because it took me a decade to even reach that point of self-love luxury.

I think as a society in general we undervalue selfishness; we are always taught and told to live selflessly and in many ways I always have, until I had nothing left to give and I realized, that, selfishness may just yet be, the greatest act of self love and self preservation of all. Why condemn ourselves for acting in the best interest of one's self? When one's self, is truly, all we have, and the greatest gift we could ever give ourselves is to be true to ourselves at all costs.

Once Upon A Candid Conversation With Myself

In order to break the cycle,
You have to be committed to breaking
The cycle; you can't just break up with someone
Then jump into the next new relationship;
You have to first honor your own brokenness,
Examine why you make the choices you make,
Have the resolve/determination to make changes
In your own self/life first, or you will continue to attract and accept and tolerate the same sort of people and behaviors you've always attracted and accepted and tolerated. We all, collectively, can raise our standards, can demand better, can expect respect; and we all collectively, can cast our fear aside and stand in our power, OUR own individual power, not the "false" sense of "power" or "acceptance" or "love" or "dopamine" we feel when someone has a crush on us; no it goes deeper than that; we ourselves, are imperfect, and in order to bring your best foot forward, and to bring YOUR best to the table, that's all anyone should really be focused on; what do you have to offer; and what are you doing, actively, right now, to commit to your own happiness. And I don't mean, cheap, easy to get happiness; I mean the happiness that only comes with being brave enough to sit with your sorrow for so long, that it no longer feels like a punishment but more like a reward; Happiness is on the other side of the hurting; you just have to be willing to be productive and to be proactively reconstructive during the time it takes to get there.

The Temptress Trope

Honestly, and this is probably just the sourpuss prude in me. Or the feminist. But I just feel like the edgy hardcore rough around the edges temptress trope is overdone. And I hate how women are generally classified into one of two categories – the innocent/pures, and the unconfined vixens. There's never any middle ground with this kind of linear thinking/labels. The character casting is outdated. Sure, a woman stroking a cigar might be a sexy aesthetic. But what's new about that? These women are a dime a dozen. Anyone can put on a pair of f&%king bad girl heels and say that they're tough as nails. But like, goddamn, where's the fun in that? The originality? The authenticity? Show me the girl who can stay high off of life itself, without any external factors or influence; I'm bored with the girl who's just pretending to cope with temporary fixes, give me Little Miss F&%king Thriving on Longterm Solutions. who's a f&%king badass not because life is easy or so damn grande, but because she doesn't need life to be some grand illusion, in order to make a grand adventure of the everyday mundane. Show me that kind of magic. Does it even exist? Show me the girl who doesn't need two glasses of wine at the table and two cigars to complete her; show me the girl who's complete being the only goddamn one at the table. Because who is this woman without the person she's tempting?

She's no one; her entire identity is the Temptress; built upon the act of tempting the other; yea her legs look good, but can she f&%king stand on them? I'm no longer impressed seeing the girl who finds new ways to numb her old pain; show me the girl who makes Pain her Lover, unabashedly, and unafraid, because Pain is her bitch and not the other way around. Show me that girl. Then that'll be someone worth jumping off the precipice for.

Next time a Man Makes you feel Small

When a man makes you feel small,
and I don't mean in the "aww look at the
cute way your hand fits into mine" or "hey
you're the perfect size to be the little spoon" way
I mean when a man makes you feel small,

like you have to lower to your voice to whispers
just for him to listen to you, or you have to
crawl back into the box he's built for you
just so he can carry
you around in his expectations,
when a man makes you feel small,
like you have to amputate entire pieces of
your soul
just to be able to stand beside
his ego,
like you have to filter out the best parts of you,
the passion, the rage, the untamed ferocity of being
alive,
just so he doesn't feel threatened
in his life...
when you've been sitting down for far too long,
because he's not ready for you to stand up for
yourself...

Next time a man makes you feel small,
instead of shrinking back into the shell or your former
self to make him comfortable, tell him that you will
no longer tear yourself in half just so he can feel whole,

if he feels threatened by how large your shadow is cast
over his floor, tell him that it took you ten years to even
tame your demons into those shadows
that now worship the ground you walk on

Next time a man makes you feel small,
tell him that you have lightning in your veins and that
every time you cry it rains and that, that kind of power
shouldn't be taken lightly,

tell him you owe it to the world to dance in
the forest naked, laughing at all the men like him who
don't understand how to speak the language of fire as it
burns and twists and sways,

tell him that your voice will never again be silenced, that
if your voice lures men to the deaths of their own pride
then yes you are a siren and yes
you are proud of it, because after finally consuming
enough half-empty souls
you realize the only person you are here to please is
yourself, and you will feed that hunger, if that
displeases others then tell the others that their approval
is no longer the shackles around
your ankles,

that only men have an Achille's heel, that Eve never
regretted eating the apple
but clearly Adam did that's why it's stuck in his throat,
tell him that the women who don't give a shit about the
rest of the world are the ones who are going to change
it,

tell him that you're not afraid of your mistakes because
every brick laid from a failed foundation paved the way
to your pedestal,

tell him
you're a woman that knows
the weight of her worth,

who knows that volcanoes have been waiting for
centuries for you to
tell them that it's a sin to be dormant for too long,

that hurricanes brew in the gulf every time you water
yourself down because someone else is thirsty for a
lesser draught of your love,

that the moon's cycle and your womb's cycle is both
29.5 days and that, that's not a coincidence that you
have that sort of pull over the universe,

tell them to put away their sword before they hurt
themselves with it- that only women wield more wiles
than wild, that while they are so busy trying to rape kill
pillage and destroy life, that only you can create it--
create LIFE-- and yet they still want to tell us how to
live, no never again, tell them that
the problem with
putting women into boxes
is that we will eventually claw our way
out of the yellow wallpaper
with our bare teeth if we have to,
and that when we do,

we will make beggars out of kings,

fools out of wise men,

and examples out of every man who told us:

        "I can only love you if you stay small."

"The Wrong Time"

There will never be a right time.
To take that leap of faith.

To do what scares you.

To tell the truth.

To confess your love.

There will be a million wrong times.

But you'd be in the wrong
if at the end of your life
You realized you refused to try
because you were so worried
about what other people thought
was wrong or right in your life
that you never took the time to
right the wrongs of each passing
Bell as it chimes, the time is now,

The time is now.

In Case No One Has Ever Told You These Truths:

A Personal Manifesto

1. I am not responsible for other people's emotions, reactions, or perceptions.
2. I am however responsible for defending my energy and guarding myself from any emotions/reactions/or perceptions that do not feel aligned with my greater good/growth.
3. My feelings are valid, they matter, and I don't have to hold them in, they deserve to be voiced in ways that are coherent, calm, and rationally discussed.
4. I am proud of myself for not being a doormat anymore, and for not prioritizing "keeping the peace" over "speaking my own truth" or for finding the strength to "stand up for myself when I feel I've been disrespected or devalued"
5. I am proud of myself for not avoiding confrontation anymore, but also for handling confrontation in a mature communicative manner (avoiding you/blame statements, acknowledging exactly where my own past traumas and perceptions come into play and working to counteract those negative behavioral patterns and viewpoints on my own without expecting others to do the dirty work for me, speaking in calm/rational ways about what I'm struggling with and discussing why logically versus not just coming out of a place of raw chaotic emotion/action).
6. I am proud of myself for not apologizing during my honesty, and for not viewing myself as weak or needy for having concerns. I respect the statements that I make, and I make them intentionally.
7. I am proud of myself for being independent enough to not have to live in fear of "losing someone" even someone "I love" because I ultimately love myself the

most out of everyone, and always want what's best for me, first and foremost, unapologetically. I will not lose myself, ever, again.
8. I know that I am strong, resilient, independent, and capable. I know that no one else defines me. And I know that this loss does not define me. I will do what I have always done; shake it off, move forward with a smile and even more growth/knowledge in my arsenal; refine further exactly what it is I'm wanting/looking for in a relationship and accept nothing less than that.
9. I am constantly evolving, and am capable of cultivating and attracting a healthy, balanced, reciprocated, equal, relationship.
10. Even though I'm very understanding and empathetic, I do not have to make excuses for people's behavior, or give them second/third/fourth chances.
11. I am allowed to express what I am unhappy with and to explain why I'm unhappy with it.
12. Conversely, other people are allowed to be mad at me, and it's not the end of the world either. I am capable of viewing multiple sides/perspectives, validating other's opinions, and continuing to work on my own self-improvement in the process; constructive criticism or feedback over things I can change (like emotional responses) are always welcome; deconstructive criticism over things I can't change (like certain health issues) however, do not need to be brought up time and time again. At that point it's not even brutal honesty, it's just needless cruelty. Either accept my reality, or don't, but get out of the middle lane; while I work on creating the life I deserve.
13. Other people's reactions/perceptions to the truth that I express, does not make my own truth any less valid; I am an adult now, and can recognize signs of gaslighting,

evasion, aversion, dishonesty, or misplaced defensiveness. I do not have to second-guess myself or the way that I feel/think/or speak, when I know that I typically feel/think long and hard about something before I even speak, so when I do speak, I know that there is some verifiable justification to it and to the process of me reaching certain conclusions.
14. I can trust my own gut and my own intuition now; if something feels unsafe, or unsuitable, or unsustainable, I am allowed to remove myself from the situation at any time.
15. I am worthy of love, and I would make a damn good partner to anyone, like they would be lucky to be with me; I know I have a few defects, maybe a little baggage I'm still clearing out, but I also know that no one is perfect, and that I am one of the chillest/coolest/stablest/kindest/mostgiving/creative/funloving/hilarious/selfless/intelligent/talented/sexiest/maturest/deepest/realest/loyalest/honestest/badassest/balancedest people ever to have in your corner.
16. I deserve respect and reciprocation. I deserve consistency and stability and harmony and maturity.
17. I value self-awareness and emotional intelligence in others. I value people who don't feign perfection but who are constantly working on their own self-growth and who are honest about the struggles they face.
18. My happiness is not now nor has it ever been dependent on anyone external; and I've already proven time and time again I have the balls to walk away from all that which does not serve me or bring out the best in me. Everytime I walk away I upgrade. Life gets better and better with every chain I break, and I don't have to regret the decisions I've made or will continue to make, because every part of it, has made me, who I am.

19. It is not other people's job to make me happy, keep me happy, or make sure I'm happy; but if someone is consistently making me mad (which takes a lot) or constantly making me feel sad, or guilty, or drained, I am allowed to carve out my own space to decide how I'm going to deal with that; to increase self-care/self-improvement time; or to cut cords if necessary.
20. In addition, it is NOT my job to make other people happy, in any way shape or form. Their expectations of me, do not matter, their desires, or wants or needs, are not more important than my own. It is okay if I "disappoint" others in some way, if it means putting myself first.
21. I do not have to give, more than I am comfortable giving. I don't have to give at all. My worth and value are not dependent on what I have to give, in any capacity.
22. I do not have to feel that my desire for depth in communication or my desire for connection makes me inherently needy or clingy; I do not have to feel guilty for wanting the things I want, or valuing the things I value even in a society that may have lost touch with these values; I just have to hold out for someone who can realistically provide that or be willing to meet me halfway.
23. I am allowed to say no.
At any time, for any reason, with no explanation necessary. And to have that no, respected, heard, understood, and upheld.
24. I am allowed to constantly evaluate and re-evaluate what I want out of life, and I have a right to assess if I am living/acting as the best version of myself in the relationships/interactions around me.
25. Being honest about my past and how it affects me in the present, is not the same thing as letting my past define my future.

26. My sole purpose in life does not have to revolve around my ability to produce offspring. I have more to offer the world than my womb, and any man who makes me believe otherwise, isn't man enough for me to begin with.
27. I am allowed to take things slow and set my own pace.
28. I am creating an inner sanctuary, and it's okay if I'm selective about who I allow in my energetic field. Having high standards is not the same thing as having impossible standards. I recognize that no one is perfect, and that I should be understanding/patient with people on their own journeys of growth and enlightenment; however, I also am aware of which particular imperfections in others that I am unable to compromise on.
29. Regardless of what others say/think about me or my reputation, I am not weak.
30. Voicing the areas in which I am hurting, is not immaturity or does not denote an inability to hold a worthwhile relationship. I am not a naggy or complainey person in general, so if I do take time to file a grievance, I don't have to second-guess myself in whether or not I should have done it in the first place; instead, I am allowed to be self-assured, and know that I did what I think was best for me, at any given time.
31. I am not broken. I am healing. Sometimes that takes time, and that's okay to take that time.
32. I respect myself, and I ultimately teach others how to treat me. It is more than okay if I do not accept or continue to accept less than desirable treatment, disrespectful interactions, or deceitful intentions. I deserve to be able to set boundaries in my life and have those boundaries respected. I deserve to be able to say no, whenever I want, no explanation necessary, in order to honor my own wants/needs.

33. I deserve to be around people who uplift my soul, not drain it.
34. I deserve to be in a romantic partnership with someone who values my time/attention/affection/effort, and who also reciprocates the same time/attention/affection/effort with the same enthusiasm and authenticity.
35. I am worth more than having to beg for anyone's attention.
36. I deserve to be with a romantic partner who notices when I am in the room, and who enjoys spending time with me. I deserve to follow my own happiness, even if it means I am unable to make everyone else around me happy in the process. I deserve to be with a romantic partner that I can experience true intimacy with, where we have a system of healthy emotional connection, trust, and communication.
37. I deserve to be with a romantic partner who will meet me halfway and put in the effort, so that it's not a one-sided relationship. I deserve to be with a romantic partner who listens to my concerns and takes them seriously. I deserve to be with a romantic partner who doesn't reject me constantly.
38. I deserve to be with a romantic partner whose actions align with their words.
39. I want to not have to explain my decisions to anyone or anybody. I want to not have to be understood, but to instead work on understanding myself well enough to be comfortable not having to validate my life choices. I deserve to put myself first for once. It's not selfish, it's life-saving.
40. I want to break old habits and patterns of thought that no longer serve me, and I want to work on becoming the best most authentic version of myself possible. I need to

know my own worth, and not settle, and not allow everyone else to tell me how to live my life.
41. I want to love myself more. To not be so hard on myself. To not be such a perfectionist. To not compare myself to others.
42. I deserve to be with a romantic partner who respects and values my life/health, and who is willing to adapt future goals/plans so that it benefits us both; and in ways that accept me as I am.
43. I deserve to heal on all levels, physically, mentally, emotionally, and psychologically. I want to help and heal others, but I first need to take steps to help and heal myself.

"Moving Forward"

I think

    all I have left is my charm and my alchemy

but I know

    that's more than enough.

What if I stopped apologizing
      for my existence,

and started living
      Unapologetically;

What if I got out of my own way,
      and started to do everything

            I was too scared to do initially;
              What if I, instead,

                    bared
                    my
                    soul
                    for
                    all
                    to
                    see,

Why Poets Do Poetry

Maybe on a subconscious level there's some part of me, (the part that is connected to all universal things) that thinks this has to be worth pursuing....

Or else, all the suffering would've been for nothing. If we, as humans, don't have a way to process our pain, to make it worthwhile, to let it grow into something even bigger than ourselves, to help others find a salve for their pain, similar to my own, then was the pain I experienced and endured even worth it.

Something has to be born from the death of us.

I'm not letting anything I went through in life, go to waste; and, I always want to push you and challenge you to do the same. Call it redemption, revenge, whatever you will, but just start and keep going. Small steps add up. Consistent action adds up. Find people who hold you accountable for your own growth.

Find your voice. Then help other people-- find theirs.

"Waiting to Ignite"

I am the embodiment of the sound a match makes
when the friction gives way to flame

Waking Fire

She was always a dragon
but now, after awakening,
she finally started
acting like one; no longer
waiting for lesser men to
wander their way into the
caves and caverns of her heart
with their arrows in hand;
No, now, she went forth boldly,
blazingly, scorchingly, torching
everything she touched;
Finally, at one, with her true
Nature, leaving nothing but
piles of bones in the wake
of her fire.

"Crimson"

There was a revolution
waking up in her bones,
as sure as fire on a flint,
sparking Red as the new day
Dawned.

~it is the hardest thing in the world
to sit with our pain
and our triggers
long enough to look them in the face,
long enough to make loneliness look like enlightenment,
long enough to uncover the parts of ourselves we've
kept hidden,

it is the hardest thing in the world
to sit with our pain
and our triggers
in order to transform them,
but it is possible,
and it is time,
to transcend.

~Life is too short to not live courageously and passionately~

~There is magic all around us,
you just have to be brave enough
to dance with it ~

~once you've mastered the art
of embodying the state of literal un-bothered-ness,
then life is yours to paint any which way you want~

About the Author

Kate Hodnett's first word as a baby was not "mama" or "dada" but was "balloon." She's not here to play around, but came out the womb hell-bent on taking flight with a head full of hot air and big ideas.
Formally, she graduated with a degree in English Arts & Humanities, and she was voted one of Louisiana's Best Emerging Poets in 2018 & again in 2019 through an anthology with Zpublishing House. Nowadays, she prefers to self-publish because if you want something done right, you do it yourself (that, or control issues, according to ya know, licensed therapists' opinions).

Informally, you can feel free to follow her as she follows her dreams on her Youtube Channel by the same name Kate Hodnett, where she shares even more poetry/art/and spoken word masterpieces, as well as details about her life with chronic illness, while sharing the battle to heal herself, others, and the world around her.

Or follow her on TikTok as username Kate Hodnett where she shares tidbits of her writing, illustrations, and love for all things nature. You can also find her original art-work & poetry pieces for sale on Etsy under TheAsterArtistStore, in addition to floral necklaces and other witchy remedies from herbal oils to tarot to self-empowerment jewelry.

What she wants out of life, more than anything, is to pursue her passion of art and poetry. And to live a peaceful witchy life, in an isolated cabin in the woods, full of love, magic, adventures, defeated fears, and profoundly immeasurable happiness.

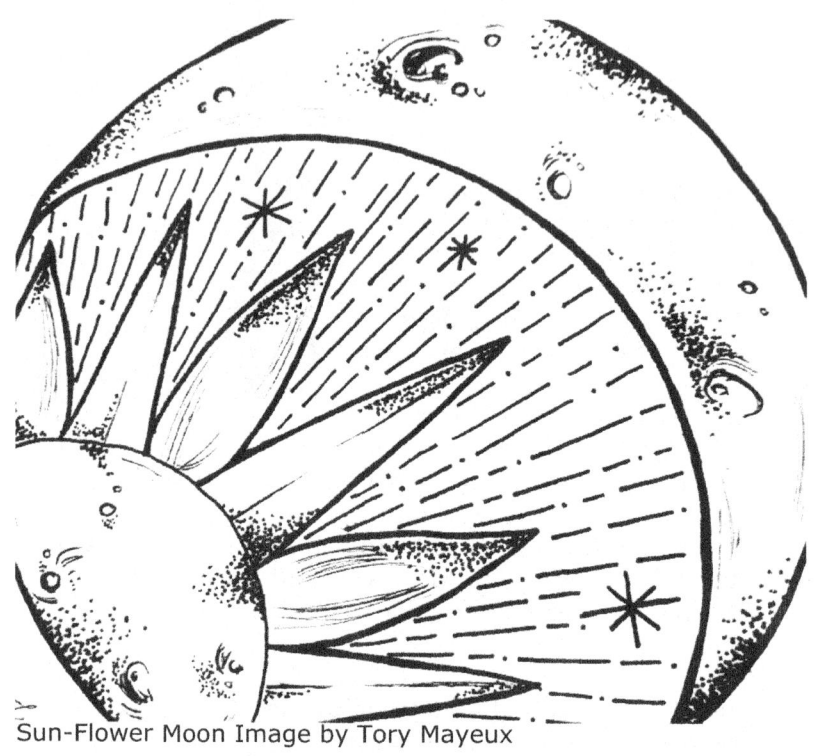
Sun-Flower Moon Image by Tory Mayeux

In loving memory of Artie Braud,

(one of the strongest, most beautiful, independent, graceful, intelligent, courageous, self-assured, confident, kind women I have ever had the pleasure of knowing)

Wish you were here to see my balls drop, sis, couldn't have done it without you.

And Janet Bailey,

It's back breaking work to break generational cycles, but if anyone's "stupid" enough to do it, I'm glad it's me. Your independence and work ethic live on, and I wish you were here to raise hell with me. But since you're not, this haphazard book will just have to suffice.

Reviews:

Don't forget to go leave a book review
on Amazon.com!

 If you would rather set yourself on fire than read this book again, or if you'd rather just set the book itself on fire. That works too. May I suggest by the light of the next full moon?

 If you thought this book was comparable to going to a fancy sushi restaurant and accidentally eating the wasabi green gum thing in one bite and being like "this tastes awful" worst chef's ever, but really it's not the chef's problem that you're an idiot.

If you like my style, kinda, in a pity-like sort of way; like when the cool kids invite you to sit at their lunch table because they feel bad for you, but like, maybe they see potential there, maybe not, maybe you're the Red Herring versus the Cady Herring. Maybe there will be a sequel, who knows.

If you liked me enough to take me home to meet your mother. I'll bring potato-salad.

Five stars if you think I'm the love-child of Shakespeare and Sylvia Plath, or maybe an Emily Dickinson/Dante combo, and you want my autograph hanging above your fireplace mantle in one of those large gold embellished Victorian-style frames.

Made in the USA
Coppell, TX
13 September 2025

FOREWORD

Myth and memory: two types of storytelling that seep into our bones and shape who we are and the world around us. The words evoke pictures of often-times small moments that have created a lasting impact. Stories so powerful that, for generations, they are shared across kitchen tables, around campfires, in rousing speeches, and of course, in the pages of books.

I can't think of a more appropriate title for this collection of short stories from ten rising young creatives.

These authors are from the ranks of The Author Conservatory, an online college-alternative program focused on writing craft and entrepreneurship, which I co-founded with Brett Harris.

Each and every one of them has fought hard to reach this milestone of publication. As with many prominent mythological figures, they have braved a strength-testing apprenticeship alongside their fellow brave students, facing critique, rejection, and seemingly impossible challenges. And every step, they have conquered fears, picked themselves up after trials, and persevered.

The students featured in this collection have graduated or are nearing graduation. As they prepare to launch their careers with serious momentum, here are a few highlights of their accomplishments:

- Several have already won or finalized for writing awards

- Most have attended professional writing conferences

- Many already have interest from agents and publishers

- All are experienced working with professional editors and on deadline

- All have extensive training in business and marketing that they have already begun to utilize

The book you are holding in your hands right now is just the beginning of their impact. Not only will they continue to grow as human beings, but their stories will bloom, too. As they are shared across kitchen tables, around coffee shops, and in rousing speeches, they will only continue to touch more and more hearts. And it all started in the pages of this book.

Like any good story, our heroes can't go it alone. They need a team–a found family–to come around and uplift them. You are a part of that. Thank you for supporting them in their journey by purchasing a copy of their collection. The proceeds of each sale go towards helping them and their classmates attend writing conferences and pursue their dreams of getting their novels in the hands of literary agents and publishers.

On behalf of the ten student authors, my co-founder Brett Harris, and our entire team of award-winning authors, professional editors, and successful entrepreneurs, thank you for investing in the voices of the future.

Because who can possibly imagine what these young writers will become?

Kara Swanson Matsumoto
Award-winning author of the Heirs of Neverland series
President of the Author Conservatory

Yes, Winie could turn to mush. *Mushy pulp, like mashed potatoes.* The thought made her shudder.

But what other choice did they have? Night would come soon, and Hazel hated the dark.

Winie pressed a paper hand on Hazel's wounded leg, careful not to touch the bleeding parts. Fear ate at the edges of Winie's paper soul like a troop of pesky termites. But it couldn't burn out the truth that blossomed like the brightest sunflower in her world: she cared about no one more than her human.

"You need help," Winie whispered. As blood continued to leak from Hazel's wound, she hoped that her human could see that, too.

Hazel took a shaking breath and pressed her lips tight. Winie knew that look. It was the look that Hazel got when she pulled at stubborn weeds in her garden or tried to loop a tricky stitch when mending her stockings.

Hazel met Winie's paper eyes. "You'll need something to protect you from the rain. Will you hand me my scissors?"

Hazel pulled her gardening glove from her overalls pocket, bright as sundrops, and laid it on the wet dirt. The fingers of the glove were still earth-stained from Hazel's garden that morning, pulling up the carrots and onion bulbs to help Mama make stew for supper.

Winie pushed the dull gardening scissors, dotted with spots of rust and vegetable strands, into the hands of her human.

If Hazel excelled at anything more than gardening, it was making Winie all sorts of dresses. Once, Hazel made Winie a suit of aluminum foil from the kitchen and pretended Winie was an astronaut ready to launch to the moon. Winie was the luckiest paper doll. Her dresses were always hung in similar patterns of color, beside skirts of fabric made from Hazel's meticulous fingers. Oh, how Winie wished she could be made of fabric, too, and not so fragile all the time.

Hopefully, whatever Hazel was making would keep her paper body from turning to mush.

Long enough to find the neighbors, at least.

Hazel's tongue pressed against her lips as she twisted the scissors in a final arc, pieces of the glove falling like spirals of lemon peels to the ground.

She set down the scissors and smiled. "The glove is rubber on top, so the rain should run straight off."

Hazel slipped the glove over Winie.

Winie winced as her paper head folded back before popping out of the rubber glove. The rest of the material nestled snug against her as she slipped her paper arms through the finger slots, now makeshift sleeves. Hazel then brought up a flap of rubber fabric behind Winie's head as a hood to keep Winie's paper curls safe.

Winie looked down at her new outfit and twirled in the drizzle. The sleeves were a bit big, but she was protected from the rain. A gleeful hope unfurled like a butterfly inside her heart, but was soon cocooned by the gloom of uncertainty.

Would the raincoat be enough to keep her paper frame dry?

What if she couldn't do this?

Winie's insides leapt like a dozen horrid grasshoppers as Hazel lifted her from the ground. She pressed her nose to Winie's cheek, and as Winie snuggled close to her human, a warmth filled the place where the coldness of fear had been moments before.

"I believe in you, Winie. Are you ready?"

Reminded of her motivation, to help her human to safety, Winie nodded.

Hazel lifted Winie to the rope.

MONSTER IN THE WOODS

Winie wrung her paper hands as she took a step away from the edge of the well, then another, then another, farther into the depths of the forest.

Woodpeckers pounded the branches. Pinecones dropped to the mossy floor. Squirrels poked their noses from their burrows inside tree trunks. The brightness of the woodland before was now snuffed in the sudden doubt that rattled Winie's paper bones.

Step after step. One at a time.

She could do this. Right?

The rain pattered down harder. Winie was careful to mind the growing puddles on the ground as she hopped from one dry patch of lichen to another.

MEGAN AMOR

M egan Amor grew up typing on her vintage typewriter late into the night, keeping her family awake with the click of the keys. Now she writes fast-paced stories with whimsical worlds that give youth a safe place to settle into their young adult shoes. She loves to remind readers of the magic of childhood while they navigate growing up.

Megan is a firm believer that dog kisses can cure any book hangover. When she's not writing she loves playing board games with her family, sipping peppermint tea, growing pumpkins in her garden, scrapbooking with old postcards, and capturing her life story with her camera.

Achievements

- Has written over six young adult fantasy novels in the last five years, along with a short story and flash fiction.

- From ages six to twelve she wrote five short stories that won first and second place award medals for the Young Author's Competition.

- Received direct guidance through paid mentorship with professional author Victoria Mccombs.

- Sent two novels to professional editors for edit letters and met multiple deadlines.

- Has attended three Writer's Conferences and received interest from agents and publishers.

- Built a photography business and practiced marketing, branding, email marketing and platform building.

Pitches

- *Spirited Away* meets *The Nightmare Before Christmas* in a YA Fantasy novel about a magical dream-land carnival and a curse that brings two siblings and a pumpkin king together in an epic chase to find three enchanted pumpkin seeds.

- *Kiki's Delivery Service* meets *Caraval* in a 1920's New York inspired YA Fantasy novel about an orphaned delivery girl who randomly starts turning into a black cat and joins a delivery contest to save her business from ruin.

At the Crossroads of Adventure
Karissa Chmil

Thickly-wooded mountains speared the sky. Herders' songs echoed off their rocky cliffs, hushing whenever the *whirr* of dragon wings passed them by.

At the foot of one of the mountains, a boy nestled a raspberry into the basket sitting in the grass at his feet.

There.

Terrence took a moment to grin down at his mound of berries. *Maybe this is how dragons feel when they look at their gold.* He snorted at the thought.

I should mention that in my next letter to Cayden. He'd like it.

Terrence plucked one more raspberry from its dark green stem and popped it into his mouth, savoring the tart sweetness. Then he leaned down to pick up his basket.

A bright saxifrage caught his eye, and he paused, brushing a gentle finger across the flower's red petals. They were Cayden's favorite, but they hadn't started blooming until two months after he left.

Terrence picked the flower, threading the stem through the woven handle of the basket. It almost made it seem like his older brother was still at home, instead of off having adventures.

He set off towards the nearest door of the inn, his soft steps on grass fading to the sharper sound of boots on cobblestones. He kept his eyes fixed on the basket held gingerly in front of him.

Spilling these now would be a catastrophe.

At the threshold, he slowed, throwing one suspicious look at his raspberries before easing the heavy wooden door open to poke his head through and look around.

His eyes fell on Sir Lanir sitting in the corner with his arms crossed, a glass of cherry brew on the table before him. His eyes were closed.

"Sir Lanir," Terrence whispered. The door began swinging shut, and he caught it with his shoulder and a soft "oof."

The old knight's eyelids fluttered open. "Eh? What's that?" His eyes roamed the room before landing on Terrence still pressed into the crack in the door. "Terrence?"

"It's me," Terrence said, still whispering. "Is Mum around?"

Sir Lanir looked around again. The weight of the door against Terrence's shoulder grew heavier, and sweat dampened the back of his neck.

The knight shook his head. "She stepped out the front just a minute ago." He squinted at Terrence. "What are you doing?"

Terrence heaved the door open and stepped into the inn with a relieved sigh. "Sneaking." He flashed a grin. "Aunt Iris is making raspberry-chocolate cake for Mum's birthday, but it's supposed to be a surprise."

"Ahhh. I see." Some far-off echo of a smile crossed the knight's face as Terrence set off across the sun-filled dining room, aiming for the swinging door to the kitchen. He kept his gaze on his pile of raspberries, intent on not letting a single one fall to the smooth wooden floor.

As he sneaked, his ears caught sounds threading through the dining room. Laughter arose from a table near the front door as men lifted glasses of chilled mint tea and clinked them together with ringing revelry. Closer to Terrence, three younger men he didn't recognize leaned in around a table, whispering big, strong words like *goblins* and *gold* and *gallant*.

He wasn't even sure what that last word meant, but as it fell from the lips of the tale-telling travelers, it rang of adventure.

And they had *swords*.

Terrence's gaze strayed from his bright red berries to admire the weapons, gleaming in the sun, long and slender.

I need a sword.

You could do important things with swords—even kill dragons, if you were brave and strong enough, and save whomever the dragons were attacking. And if you did important things, you were a hero.

A raspberry began rolling down the pile, and he jumped, tearing his gaze away from the swords just in time to catch it.

He pressed his tongue against his teeth and hurried towards the kitchen before any more near-disasters. The raspberry looked guilty, and he huffed under his breath at it. It was rude, interrupting someone when they were thinking about important things like swords.

Getting one would be easier if Cayden was still at the inn. Brothers were easier to convince about swords than mothers or aunts.

If I had a sword, then I could be a hero. It made *sense*, but somehow he didn't think that would convince them.

Terrence pushed through the swinging door.

Aunt Iris turned from the counter. Sunlight slanted in from the kitchen window, lighting up her smile. Wisps of brown hair, unmarked by the gray streaks in Mum's hair, had escaped the braids pinned around her head. "You succeeded!"

Terrence crossed the small room and set his basket on the counter beside her. He released a breath and returned her smile. "I did! Though I should have used a bigger basket." He started unthreading the flower from the handle to give to Mum when he saw her.

She laughed. "This cake's just meant for the three of us, Terrence. We don't need to feed the entire town." She turned back to the counter, where shavings of chocolate sat beside a bowl of thick, dark batter. "Could you juice a couple lemons for me?"

Terrence set the flower near the basket, taste-tested a small bit of the chocolate, and dodged Aunt Iris' friendly glare. He reached towards a bowl of fruit under the hanging pots and pans and pulled out a lemon.

"I wish it was for the four of us," he said softly. He brightened. "Could we send a piece to Cayden?"

The soft scritch-scratch of Aunt Iris' knife against the chocolate paused. "It might not stay good that long, Terrence. Didn't his last letter say something about the Chana mountains?"

Terrence sagged. "I think so." If Cayden and Sir Andrius did climb the Chana mountains and cross the river, their cake would be dry as sand by the time it reached him.

He sighed and reached for a knife.

His fingers curled around the handle, and he eyed it critically. Knives were somewhat like swords. *And* they were useful. Maybe that would convince Mum and Aunt Iris to let him get a sword. Maybe, if all the knives were dirty, he could just—

"Terrence?" Aunt Iris' voice broke into his vision of swords, of coming to the rescue when none of the knives were available and cutting bread for a really important hero who needed to eat right *then* so that he could go fight a griffin. Or whatever else a hero did on a normal afternoon.

"Yes?"

She wiped her hands on a towel, then reached into the pocket of her skirt. "I meant to give this to you yesterday. Will you still have time to make Mum's wreath before dinner, like you wanted?" She dropped a ball of brown twine in his hand.

Terrence turned it over. "Oh. Probably." The ball felt so small in his hand, and he sighed. *Making a wreath of flowers isn't very heroic.*

"Iris! Terrence!" Mum's voice flew before her.

Aunt Iris had just enough time to slap a bowl over the pile of chocolate shavings while Terrence threw a towel over the basket of raspberries before Mum burst into the kitchen. Her cheeks shone, like she'd been crying, but a smile stretched across her face with the light of spring sunshine dripping through new leaves.

And there was someone following her, wearing the griffin-hide boots Terrence's father used to wear—

"Cayden?"

Terrence and Aunt Iris' voices collided with each other. Then Terrence gasped at his brother, and Aunt Iris sprang forward to wrap Cayden in a hug.

When she stepped back a minute later, she was laughing and wiping her eyes.

"Oh, you rascal, why didn't you *tell* us you were coming home?"

"I didn't know," Cayden said, his blue eyes seeming to laugh with her. "Sir Andrius didn't expect the summer floods to make the river impassable this early, so we came back to wait them out." His eyes landed on Terrence. "Hail, Prince Terrence."

"Hail, King Cayden," Terrence responded in a daze.

His brother had left to accompany Sir Andrius on the knight's adventures only three months ago, but it had been a very long, very dreary three months since they had climbed trees and fought with sticks as King Cayden and Prince Terrence. "You're... back! In time to..." He trailed off, just keeping himself from blurting something about the cake and ruining the surprise. "You're back for Mum's birthday!" he amended.

Cayden winked. "I am! And I have something for the occasion." He dug into his satchel and pulled out a small object, wrapped in red cloth. He handed it to his mother. "Happy birthday, Mum."

Her eyes misted over. "You didn't have to, Cayden. You've been traveling."

"I wanted to."

Mum gently unfolded the fabric and gasped, holding it out on a flat palm.

Terrence stood on his tiptoes to see it.

Mum lifted it with the tips of her fingers. It was smaller than one of Terrence's fists, and it glimmered blue-green in the sunlight. "Is this...?"

"A dragon scale? Yes, ma'am." Cayden smiled sheepishly, leaning back on the counter beside Terrence.

"You killed a *dragon*?" Terrence's voice squeaked. Cayden had killed a dragon! He had stopped it from burning houses and hurting families, and something about his brother's sun-darkened figure seemed stronger now.

Pink flushed Cayden's cheeks. "Only a small one."

Mum looked up from her present and rested a hand against Cayden's cheek. "Thank you, son. You've made me proud." She laughed and shook her head. "Terrified for you, but so proud."

"A hero," Aunt Iris said, her eyes dancing and her words solemn and glad all at once. "Our Cayden's a hero." Then she pursed her lips in the way that said she wasn't angry, just worried. "Possibly an idiotic one—a *dragon*, Cayden?—but still. A hero."

Cayden ducked his head after Mum drew her hand back. "I suppose so." He looked around and sighed, a long, happy sound. "Oh, it's *good* to be home."

Then his brow furrowed. Terrence followed his brother's gaze and looked up at the windowsill, finely layered with dust.

"I was supposed to dust that yesterday," Terrence mumbled.

Cayden looked at him with a distracted smile, eyes flicking to the windowsill again. "Where are Mum's flowers, Terrence?" His voice was low. "From our meadow?"

Terrence half-shrugged. "We haven't been to the meadow in a while." Other springs, the inn had brimmed with the flowers Mum brought home after family excursions to the little meadow tucked behind the inn. But not this year.

Cayden looked up at the windowsill, and some of the laughter faded from his eyes.

"Now, tell us all about your adventures, Cayden." Aunt Iris' voice drew the boys' attention back to the other side of the kitchen. "Did you go up the Chana mountains after all?"

"Up the foothills, yes." Cayden slid his satchel off his shoulder and dropped it on the counter. "Sir Andrius knows a family there. He rescued the little girl from lions years ago, and—"

"*Lions?*" Terrence glanced back at the satchel. "Actually, really real lions?"

"Actually, really real lions." Cayden poked Terrence's shoulder. "That's what heroes do."

Mum looked back down at the dragon scale and smiled.

Terrence swallowed. His ball of twine sat on the counter next to Cayden's satchel, forgotten in all the excitement. A darting glance to the other counter showed the wilting leaf of the saxifrage peeking out from under the towel covering the basket.

I can't give her flowers after Cayden gave her a dragon scale, he thought, as Cayden, at Aunt Iris' prompting, launched into a story about a phoenix fire he and Sir Andrius had put out.

Cayden's a hero. Giving Mum flowers is too much like... me.

Story led to story, full of the same kinds of words the visiting heroes used. Dwarves and spears and a hundred other things that were bigger and stronger and more heroic than flowers.

Terrence stuffed the twine in his pocket.

I'll come up with some other idea.

He couldn't disappoint Mum by being so much less heroic than Cayden. Not on her birthday.

A sudden drumming of laughter crashed into the kitchen, and the family fell silent. Sunshine poured in through the flower-less windowsill.

Mum sighed, smoothing out her dark red skirt, the color of the saxifrage. "We've got some hungry folk out there. We'll have to finish catching up tonight."

"Duty calls," Aunt Iris agreed, stepping to the stove to stir a pot of stew.

A soft ding rose above the voices in the dining room, and Mum looked at Terrence. "Could you find out what that new guest would like? Cayden, you can take your things upstairs; you should get some rest."

"I'd like to help with the guests, if that's allowed." He sent a sideways wink at Terrence.

Mum frowned. "But you just got back."

"Exactly." He stepped towards her, saying something with his eyes that Terrence didn't understand.

Mum seemed to, though, because she nodded, her forehead smoothing out. "In that case, you and I can check on the guests already at tables." Her eyes strayed to Terrence, and her eyebrows rose. "Terrence, the new guest?"

"Oh, right." He scrambled through the swinging door and into the dining room, scanning the gathered people.

Near the far left of the room, a tall man with a dark beard was lowering himself into an empty bench.

Terrence grinned and wove his way towards him. "Master Benjen?"

The blacksmith's face lit up. "Ah, Terrence! Just the lad I wanted to see." Sunlight threaded the many black strands of his beard. His eyebrows rose when

Cayden and Mum slipped out of the kitchen, and he tilted his head. "He's back?"

Terrence nodded.

Master Benjen smiled. "I'm sure you've all been feasting on his stories."

Terrence hesitated, then nodded again.

"Speaking of feasting"—the blacksmith rubbed his hands together—"You don't happen to have any of your aunt's cauliflower stew on hand, would you?"

"We do."

The man's smile broadened. "And some sesame rolls. Thank you, lad."

Terrence turned and picked his way back towards the kitchen, noting Mum and Cayden moving from table to table and checking on the guests. Mum kept her hands folded while she asked quick, gentle questions and made sure everyone had what they needed. Cayden, on the other hand, swapped a joke with every person he passed, his eyes sparkling as he supplied empty glasses and extra spoons.

In the kitchen, Aunt Iris set to dipping up a bowl of stew from the pot simmering on the stove. While he waited, Terrence peeked into Cayden's satchel. He spied a few other cloth-wrapped items, a rolled map, and something that looked suspiciously like a dagger.

Then he took the bowl of stew and a plate of sesame rolls back out to the dining room, sighing with relief when he didn't spill anything.

Master Benjen's smile made crinkles show up around his eyes. "Ah, thank you, lad." He breathed in the steam.

A pair of hands came down and rested on Terrence's shoulders. He twisted his neck to see Mum behind him. "Good day, Master Benjen," she said.

He raised a spoonful of stew like a salute. "My compliments to the chef, mistress, as always."

Terrence could hear the smile in her voice as she thanked him. Then she said, "Terrence, I need to check in on Widow Ada. Aunt Iris says she and Cayden can handle the inn for the afternoon, so you can still run… an errand, I think she said you wanted to do?"

Flowers. Aunt Iris was talking about flowers.

Something sour churned in Terrence's stomach.

"But be back before dark." Mum leaned down and kissed his cheek, and he squirmed away.

"All right."

After another few words to Master Benjen, she slipped away.

Terrence slumped into the bench across from the blacksmith, the sour feeling still simmering inside him. "Master Benjen, did you know it's Mum's birthday?"

"Is it? Happy birthday to her!" He took another bite like a celebration.

"Mhm. And I still don't have a present for her."

"Ah." Master Benjen wiped his beard with a napkin. "Now that's a problem."

"Cayden gave her a dragon scale, and she was *very* happy," Terrence said thoughtfully. "But I think she was more happy because of him than the present. So I need to give her something that will let her know I'm a hero."

"A hero, you say?"

Something in his voice made Terrence frown. "Isn't being a hero a good thing?"

"Oh, yes, yes. A very good thing." He took another bite of stew, then said more lightly, "I'm always partial to gifts made out of metal, myself. Maybe a—"

"A sword!" Terrence shot up.

Master Benjen tapped his finger against his spoon. "Well, I was going to say a locket—"

"But swords are what heroes use," Terrence insisted. After a moment of thought, he added, "Though she might not know where to put a whole sword. Maybe just a dagger." That would be small enough for Mum to keep and still impressive enough that she would know he was a hero, which was probably what she really wanted.

Master Benjen studied Terrence, then looked down at his now-empty bowl. He pushed it across the table, then reached into his pocket and pulled out a small brass coin. He laid it beside the bowl with a clink. "All right, lad. You take this coin to your aunt to pay for the meal and"—His eyes lit up—"a lemon custard, for dessert. And if you're sure she'd want it, I'll help you make your mum a dagger."

Terrence grinned. "Oh, I'm sure." He grabbed the coin and darted off towards the kitchen.

Fifteen minutes later, he and the blacksmith strode down the sun-soaked cobblestones towards the smithy. Birds twittered in the trees alongside the road, their song quickening Terrence's steps.

Master Benjen greeted everyone they passed by name, and Terrence rippled his hands in wave after wave.

He lifted his chin, looking up at the sky, blue and punctuated by fluffy clouds. Sunshine dripped down on everything, from his shoulders to the mountains that soared up around them.

It was a good day to be a hero.

At the bottom of the hill, Master Benjen steered them off the road into the smithy. Half-made tools lay scattered across tables. Deep inside the forge, embers glowed like dragon fire.

Terrence perched on the edge of a table as Master Benjen picked up a dagger with an intricately designed hilt. "Making one of these takes a lot of patience, Terrence. You'll start with a piece of metal, get it down to size, then hammer out the blades and work on the hilt."

Terrence studied the knife. "I can do it."

Master Benjen's eyes twinkled. "Let me show you around the place and introduce you to the tools you'll be using."

Terrence hopped down from the table and trailed behind him, trying to remember each name as the man wove through his smithy, gesturing to this tool or that tool.

When he finally paused for breath, he raised his eyebrows. "A bit overwhelming, Terrence?"

"Maybe a little bit," Terrence admitted. "But I can still do it." He *had* to do it.

"That's the spirit." Master Benjen picked up a long rectangle of metal and weighed it in his hand. "This isn't easy, lad, but most good things aren't. You love your mum, right?"

Terrence nodded.

"You're ready to work to show her that?"

Terrence nodded again, and Master Benjen smiled. "Cayden should be proud to have you for a brother."

Terrence frowned. *I'm not... Cayden's the one...*

Before he could piece his thoughts back together, Master Benjen handed him the piece of metal. "Is this about the size you're thinking?"

Terrence hummed, measuring it against his hand. They were nearly the same size. "Can I have a bigger one?"

Master Benjen hesitated. "Bigger ones take more time, Terrence. You might not be able to finish—"

"I'll work fast," he promised. "Please?" He couldn't make her something the size of a letter opener. Cayden had made a dagger before he left, at least twice as big as this.

That was what a hero did.

"I'll let you try," Master Benjen said. He handed Terrence a different piece of metal. "Like that?"

Terrence nodded.

"All right. Wait a minute, and I'll..." He walked off, still talking. A moment later, he returned with a small box filled with an uneven jumble of faded paper. "Sort through this, lad, and find a knife outline that's the right size. Then"—he cast a quick look around the shop and nodded towards the door—"use that paste to attach the paper to the metal. Not too much, mind, just enough that it won't float away. Then come find me."

"Yes, sir." Terrence gripped the metal with sweaty palms. *I'm doing it. I'm actually going to be a hero.*

Master Benjen winked at him and walked off, whistling. He picked up a hammer and began pounding something as Terrence peeked into the box. Each strip of paper was the exact shape of a knife, all different lengths. They were thick, oily-looking things that left faint yellow streaks on his fingers.

Once he had selected the one he wanted, Terrence took it and the metal over to the door, finding the jar of paste Master Benjen had pointed out. He used the little brush to coat the paper, then pressed his tongue against his upper lip as he smoothed it out on the metal.

After he had done that, Master Benjen paused his hammering and came over to help cut the metal down to the right shape. Tool after tool, all with odd names, passed through Terrence's hands.

At some point, Master Benjen's apprentice came in, smiled at Terrence, and began working at the bellows. Hot air filled the smithy. Sweat beaded on Terrence's forehead.

Time blurred. Being a blacksmith, Terrence decided faintly, was a terrible idea if you didn't like loud noises or doing the same thing over and over.

Soon his ears rang from the constant echoing clanging of hammers.

Sweat ran into his eyes, and he clumsily wiped at them with an aching wrist. He had spent the last twenty minutes trying to get one side of the dagger the same shape as the other. It hadn't seemed that long when he picked the size, but now it seemed enormous. His arms were so tired, and he kept thinking about cool breezes and raspberries and—

He clenched his teeth. *It's hard. But it's supposed to be hard. I need to*—he swiped at his forehead again—*I need to show Mum that I can be a hero, too, just like*—

"Terrence?"

He started, looking up to see Master Benjen, his shadow falling across the table. The last throbbing clang faded from the smithy, leaving a silence that made room for cheerful voices and laughter to come in from the street.

"It's about time for you to head home, lad."

Terrence swallowed, looking down at his dagger. One edge was still thicker than the other, even though he'd been sanding it for longer than spriggans had lived underground. The handle mostly didn't exist, either. "But I'm not done."

"You did choose a big one," Master Benjen pointed out mildly. "You could show this to your mum tonight and come back tomorrow to keep working on it." He handed a file to his apprentice, who was moving quietly through the shop tidying tools.

"But I need to have it tonight," Terrence said, tightening his grip on the knife.

Heroes didn't *half*-rescue people; they did things all the way. "Can't I stay and keep working?"

Master Benjen put a hand on Terrence's shoulder. "I heard your mum say you should be back before dark," he said gently. "Go home, Terrence. You're welcome back tomorrow."

Terrence stumbled out of the shop, gripping the half-made dagger. His throat burned.

He stopped in the street, watching people bustle past carrying fresh bread and laughing their good evenings to each other. Inside the shop, Master Benjen's voice mixed with his apprentice's. The other boy chuckled.

Unheroic tears stung at Terrence's eyes.

All that work, all that sanding, all those dreams of giving Mum a dagger, of showing her that he was a hero too.

And now he stood here, in the sunset-brushed street, all alone.

"Terrence? Is that you?"

Terrence hastily wiped at his eyes as his brother approached. "Cayden?" His voice was scratchier than normal.

"How'd the expedition go?" Cayden asked. Orange rays of light slanted down around him and made his copper-colored hair gleam.

Terrence halfheartedly waved his dagger. "Awfully." His throat tightened again. He couldn't think of what else to say, so he mumbled, "What are you doing?"

"Picking up some streamers for Aunt Iris." Cayden held them up in the dusky light. "I thought you were making a wreath." He squinted at the dagger. "Is that for Mum?"

"It *was* for Mum," Terrence corrected, swallowing. "Can we go home?"

Cayden frowned, but after a moment, he nodded.

They set off up the hill in silence. Townspeople passed them, some welcoming Cayden home with broad smiles.

With every word, the sour feeling in Terrence's stomach dug deeper. His fingers ached.

I didn't do it. I couldn't do it. He walked without looking where he was going, lost in himself.

"Ter?" Cayden's voice broke into his thoughts halfway up the hill. He sounded hesitant.

Terrence glanced over at him.

"How did... what was the inn like while I was gone?" Cayden asked.

Terrence frowned, trying to focus on the strange question. "Quieter, I think. Aunt Iris said we should have gotten a puppy, but we didn't." He shrugged. "Still lots of visiting heroes."

"But the flowers." Cayden's voice was low. "The meadow. Terrence, why doesn't Mum have flowers in the kitchen anymore?"

"Oh." Terrence ran a thumb across the cool hilt of his knife. "The little bridge fell down, and Mum said she couldn't use the steppingstones. So we didn't go." After a moment, he added, more softly, "Picnics or walks without you wouldn't have been right anyway." He bit his lip and whispered, "Mum missed you."

Everyone had missed him.

Cayden stopped. Terrence instinctively did the same. His brother's blue eyes were soft in the growing dark. "I'm glad she still had you."

I'm glad she still had you.

Terrence stopped fingering the dagger.

Cayden shifted his streamers to one hand. "Can I look at your knife?"

Terrence handed it to him, watching as Cayden spun it over his knuckles. It fit his hand so much better than Terrence's, but of course it did, because Cayden was the one who used daggers.

Cayden was the one who killed dragons.

Not Terrence.

Cayden handed it back. "Mum needs you, Terrence." His voice was steady in the dark. "Not you pretending to be me. She needs *you*." After a moment, he kept walking.

Terrence hurried to catch up, his brother's words spinning in his mind. Yes, Mum had missed Cayden, and yes, Mum was proud of Cayden. But maybe she didn't want Terrence to *be* Cayden. Did she want him to do *Terrence* things, not Cayden things?

Strokes of pink pressed into the sky. In the west, they had faded to a blue-gray, ready to welcome the first stars.

Cayden nudged Terrence's shoulder, steering them off the road and into the grass.

"Where are we going?" Terrence asked.

"The meadow," Cayden said. "Before it gets too dark."

"It's already dark," Terrence mumbled, but he followed Cayden down the hill. They picked their way through the thickening trees, cloaked in shadows and laced with lightning bugs.

Terrence drank it in, slowly. He hadn't been to the meadow since Cayden left. None of them had, not since a rush of melting snow had knocked down the old bridge. No more family picnics. Mum had stopped filling windowsills with flowers or threading them through the buttonholes on her dress.

Cayden stopped at the edge of the creek. Terrence joined him, and they watched the water tumble by in a cacophony of blues, blacks, and whites.

"There's the old bridge," Terrence said, pointing to a plank of rotting wood jammed between two rocks.

"There it is," Cayden murmured. "You know, this sounds like the beginning of a story."

Terrence threw him a suspicious look, but he couldn't make out if Cayden was teasing in the dark.

Cayden's voice dropped low and rich, like the bards who sometimes stayed at the inn and enthralled the dining room with epic ballads. "Rushing waters threaten the warrior with the wounded blade, yet he tightens his grip. The blood of heroes sings—"

"I don't think I'll ever be a hero."

Cayden fell silent. When he spoke again, he wasn't a bard, or a king, or even a dragon-killer. He was just his brother, who slid down stairs on blankets and smuggled muffins into their room and taught his little brother how to pick out constellations in the sprawling storybook of the sky. "Why's that, Ter?"

"Because." Terrence swallowed again and waved his unfinished blade at the creek. "I can't do big things, like making daggers or using swords or killing dragons. Just... Terrence things, like picking flowers, which isn't very heroic at *all*, and—"

"Do you remember Master Gatlin, Terrence?"

Taken aback by the subject change, it took a moment for him to nod. Master Gatlin had stayed at the inn for a few months last winter, and his unseeing eyes had glimmered in the firelight with steady wonder.

"Remember how he would always give up his chair when a mother came in with a baby?"

Terrence nodded again.

"That's what a hero is." Cayden's voice was steady. "They do whatever's needed, big or small."

Whatever's needed. The words nestled into Terrence's mind.

Master Gatlin had never climbed mountains or challenged giants. He never even owned a sword. But the inn wasn't a place to do any of that. It was a place to sit and let people rest.

So if a dragon is attacking someone, then a hero's whoever stops the dragon. But if someone was hungry, a hero was whoever gave them food or chased rabbits out of a garden, or... anything.

The creek babbled at his feet. Terrence's grip loosened on his dagger.

Whatever's needed.

Mum still wanted flowers.

She couldn't cross the steppingstones, but Terrence could. He could make her a wreath and help her fill the inn with flowers again.

He *could* be a hero.

Silver light sprinkled down from the sky, lighting up every bit of Cayden's smile. "I need to go help Aunt Iris hang streamers. I'll see you at home?"

"Yeah," Terrence said. His hands quivered with excitement, the sour feeling finally gone. "I'll see you at home."

Cayden slipped away in the dark.

A choir of crickets sang in the bushes around Terrence. An owl hooted overhead like it wanted someone to join it on its journey. The creek never stopped laughing, even if no one was listening.

If anyone knew what a hero was, it was Cayden. He had traveled with Sir Andrius. He could use a sword. He had killed a dragon.

And, Terrence thought in a daze, *he's always been my hero.*

But the things that had made him Terrence's hero weren't dragons or griffins. They were the whispered stories told in secret, candle-lit meetings. They were the apples thrown down from trees Terrence was too small to climb.

They weren't *big*. But they were needed, and oh, *oh*, that's what being a hero meant.

Terrence checked to make sure he still had his ball of twine, took a deep breath, and began crossing the creek.

His boots slid across the damp moss on the first steppingstone, and he yelped, holding out his arms. When he regained his balance, thankful he'd avoided tumbling into the cold water, he stepped to the next stone. This one was drier, and a sneaky, triumphant smile started creeping onto his face.

Here and there, water lapped at his feet. Once, he had to cling to a low-hanging tree branch to keep from slipping off into the creek.

But he made it, boots wet, hands chilly, and still grinning.

On this side of the creek, the meadow stretched out in a gray-draped tangle of flowers, their colors barely distinguishable in the dark. Beneath them, Terrence liked to think, little field mice made nests and told bedtime stories.

Stars sang above him.

Terrence found a broken branch near the creek bank, then dropped to his knees and set to work. He managed to twist the branch into a circle to serve as a base, knotting it together with twine.

He used the sharper side of the dagger to cut flowers and lengths of twine, tying them into little bundles. One by one, he added them to the base, periodically cocking his head and examining it, then working in another sprig of silver thistles between the asters and meadow rues.

Finally, he held out his wreath. The flowers and ferns woven into every side glowed softly in the starlight.

Terrence smiled.

He stood, pocketed his knife and twine, and began his journey home. He held the wreath in one hand as he crossed the creek, holding his breath until he reached the opposite bank. Then he slipped through the quiet trees, and stepped back onto the street.

A few shopkeepers wished him a goodnight as they locked their doors and headed for home. Windows threw blocks of light onto the ground.

Everything was still, a thousand-thousand leagues away from the clamor of the smithy. Somehow, he decided, it was easier to breathe here.

Terrence arrived back at the inn and crept upstairs. One of the spare rooms had been claimed for the celebration, and he eased the door open and looked around.

A large fireplace filled the room with glimmering cheerfulness. Aunt Iris' cake sat on the table in all its glory, along with four plates of grilled sandwiches. Ribbon-tied streamers crisscrossed the ceiling.

Cayden stood near the door, whittling something. He looked up with a smile. "He's back!"

A chair scraped across the floor by the hearth, where Mum and Aunt Iris sat talking. "Terrence? I thought I told you to be home by dark."

Terrence let the door fall shut with a quiet click and crossed towards Mum. "I was making you this." He held out the wreath, sudden weariness seeping through him.

Mum's eyes softened as she accepted the gift, holding it gently in both hands just like she had held the dragon scale. "Oh, Terrence..."

"I made it with some flowers from our meadow," he explained, anxious to make her understand. "I thought–I thought, because you couldn't go to the meadow, because the bridge is gone, I could bring some of the meadow to you." He shifted from one foot to another. "I hope you like it."

Mum held out her arms without a word, and Terrence leaned into the hug.

Flowers tickled his cheek. He squirmed away, pressing closer into Mum.

When she finally let him go, her eyes were teary. A smile creased her face, though, as deep and real as any he could imagine. "Thank you, Terrence." She squeezed his hand.

"Prince Terrence?"

Terrence looked over at Cayden who leaned on the back of Aunt Iris' chair and rocked her gently.

"What do you say we start rebuilding a bridge tomorrow?" Cayden asked.

Terrence gasped. "Oh! Oh, *yes*, King Cayden. Yes."

Cayden and Aunt Iris laughed.

Mum only smiled. "My heroes."

Cayden winked at Terrence.

Terrence grinned.

KARISSA CHMIL

Karissa Chmil spent her childhood running through Indiana cornfields, climbing the French alps, and exploring West African savannas, learning from a young age that there is delight hidden in every corner of the world. Now she writes stories that help kids fall in love with goodness, sweeping them off on quests while showing that virtue is the greatest adventure of all. When she's living a story rather than writing one, you can find her studying foreign languages, ink drawing with fountain pens, and coddiwompling across whatever tree-ish place she can find.

Achievements

- Drafted eight novels and novellas.

- Placed as an honorable mention in the Leyla Beban Young Authors Foundation writing contest.

- Attended the Write-to-Publish conference in 2023.

- Received an edit letter on a completed manuscript.

- Interned with author Nova McBee and One Door Studios to brainstorm, develop, and implement book marketing plans.

- Has served as Community Assistant for the Young Writer's Workshop since 2021.

- Has received extensive business training and launched her own business as a teenager.

- Has received extensive email marketing training and has started a growing email list.

Pitches

- An African MG fantasy about an eleven-year-old girl who has to break her village's "one storyteller" tradition to save her friend the baobab tree and bring back the rain after a drought.

- An *Aladdin* x *Moby Dick* YA retelling about a young street rat desperate to prove he's more than his station who joins a ship sailing across the desert to kill a sand dragon.

- A MG fantasy about a twelve-year-old girl yearning to follow in her eagle-riding father's legacy despite her crippling fear of heights who treks across the jungle to recover a stolen eagle collar.

SON OF THE EVENING STAR
JAMES NOLLER

"**W**ill my Light ever come?"

The young Star on the mountain looked to the sky as his murmured question rose over the restless night breeze and up to the hundred hardworking Stars in the dark. Each one burned his brilliant, silver shield against the shadows, each one pushing back a little corner of the night.

But no answer fell back to the young, glowless Star waiting on the ground.

Charidor reached out a hand to his shining kinsmen. He'd heard their stories—of battling comets and asteroids and burning through long years alone in the cold. But even here, on the tallest mountain above his village, he could barely scrape at the great chasm that stretched between him and the silver Warriors of the sky.

Just beyond his fingertips, the brightest Star in the night—his father, the mighty Evening Star—blazed like a drop of silver fire in the dark.

"Please, Father," Charidor muttered. "Why am I the only one left?"

Darkness hovered over his fingertips.

"I should be up there with you."

His father's steady glow blurred like watercolors with the sky.

He pulled his hand back and turned his face away. He seethed out a heated breath. "Am I even a Star?"

A long, cold wind whistled in reply.

He shivered, turning to the old, hanging lantern that stood its ground on the mountain's crest. Its steady, orange fire pooled over the rocks, and the young Star huddled into its warmth.

A sharp swish rattled the nearby bushes.

Charidor whirled, scanning the shadows and leaves. Another ruffle shook the dark. He threw up his fists, fighting to steady his breath. He could hold his own, he knew, as long as he stayed in the light.

A silhouette darted from the underbrush. Charidor roared out a warning.

The lantern's bright gleam caught a shimmer of blue-and-green fur.

"Whoa, hold up! It's only me."

Charidor let his hands fall. "Pyr! Must you creep up on me in the dark?"

The slinking fox grinned. "Just caught my leg between two particularly stubborn sticks." Pyr shook his shining blue coat, but the broken twigs stuck in his fur refused to budge.

The young Star laughed, rolling his eyes. "Come, let me do it."

Pyr trotted across the lantern's amber pool and obediently placed himself under Charidor's hands. Carefully, the young Star plucked each twig from the fox's soft, iridescent coat. Half a pinecone had somehow matted itself beneath Pyr's fur. As he gently worked to free it, Charidor couldn't help but sigh.

Even Pyr had his own subtle glow, born as he was from the Aurora Ristrallas in the mountain peaks. He'd carried that same luminescent wash of blue into green, that pinkish tinge around his tail and ears, since the very first hour his paws padded the earth.

Pyr gazed up at him with great, golden eyes. "Watching the clouds come in?"

Charidor tried to smile, standing as the breeze blew cool, pine air past his cheek and murmured over the darkening forest. "Sleep refuses to fall on me tonight."

The whispering wind brushed its fingers through the distant leaves of the valley.

"Exactly twelve months have passed since Aliessa found her starglow and took up her Sky Assignment. It came sooner than anyone thought possible. She shone so bright. But me, well..." His shoulders sank. "Everyone has been waiting a long time, now."

The farthest Stars flickered in the deep darkness.

A brush of soft fur nudged at his ankles. "You'll find it. You're the son of the Evening Star. Who knows what you've got under the surface?"

Charidor glanced down at his companion and a small weight lifted from his chest. He gave his friend a gentle scratch behind the ears as the fox absently surveyed the woods, coat rippling in the wind.

Grey clouds gathered on the horizon, billowing into a dark, angry line. The great Stars, so high above, formed rank, stringing together their brilliant, silver Constellations over the sky.

"Sometimes," he murmured, "I fear I'll never be strong enough to face it."

"Face what?"

Charidor swallowed as the clouds stretched out long, black claws. "The dark."

A great wind picked up, whistling by his ear and ruffling the trees. The clouds drifted across the night, like a thick cloak. The mighty Conch Constellation rallied to face the attack, but the gathering clouds slipped silently over it, covering each Star in a long trail. The Great Bridge and the Arrow Constellations stepped up to the battleline in a fierce silver formation, but they too were swallowed by the clouds. Stars, like flickering messages, fell silent, one by one.

Charidor clenched his teeth as the clouds cut him off from his kin.

Soon, only his father, the great Evening Star, shone clear as a beacon in the final corner of the darkening sky. But he, too, slipped beyond the veil.

Charidor now stood alone.

Cold and dark covered the earth.

Gently, the lantern's soft glow lapped at Charidor's bare feet, the last defense against the shadows.

Not a leaf stirred.

A sharp cry rang out in the night and shot into Charidor's ears.

He gasped. "What was that?"

The fox tilted his ears. "What was what?"

"A shout. A cry for help. A boy. A human boy, I think, trapped in the dark."

Pyr eyed Charidor with his sharp, golden gaze. "You heard a Call."

The world blurred and spun. Charidor blinked until his vision cleared and he scanned the endless grey roof, searching for any sign of a gap. "But, no Star will have heard his cry for help through these clouds."

"You did."

The fox leaped onto a rock, ears perked and fur on edge.

Charidor shook his head. "No, I mean a real Star."

"Do you know where the Call came from?"

The young Star steadied his breath, listening into the far reaches of the wood.

"There," he said at last, pointing. "A cave lies beneath that hill over yonder."

Pyr's eyes grew to enormous orbs, fixed on Charidor. "Incredible," he muttered.

The shadows deepened over the forest. Something dark and cold pulled at the corners of Charidor's robes, beckoning, whispering behind hissing leaves.

Alone among the creatures of the night, without a Star in the sky... How would the boy last until morning?

"I have to find someone who can help." He tugged away from the shadows' grip and sprinted to the path back home.

"Wait!" Pyr called. "Where are you going?"

Charidor thundered down the steps, heedless of the steep incline. Every second cut the boy's chance of survival in that cold cave.

Two piercing howls soared over the wood, and Charidor slid to a dusty halt.

Pyr materialized at Charidor's heels. "Wolves!" His usually silky voice quavered. "Are they close?"

Charidor scanned the forest, the darkening world once more refusing to focus. "They're heading in the same direction as the boy's Call." He'd never make it now to the village before the wolves sniffed out the child.

Pyr gathered himself to full height. "We have to do something."

The young Star ran a hand over his eyes.

He didn't understand. In all his many nights walking the earth, at least one Star always stood guard against the dark, waiting to respond to a Call for help.

There is still one, a soft voice whispered by his heart.

Charidor clenched a fist. "I can't go out there. Not without my Light."

But as he searched across the mountain for an answer, the lantern's amber eye twinkled, as though it had been watching him. Its fire spilled over into Charidor's chest.

He ran for it.

"Wait! Where are you going *now*?"

Charidor pulled the lantern from its hold, thrusting its gleaming fire to the night. With a steadying breath, he bolted into the shadowed trees.

"Wait for me!" Pyr cried, his voice cracking. "You're not going in there alone!"

Charidor didn't stop. He didn't dare turn from the gleaming, amber tunnel that the lantern carved through the woods. For he knew that, right behind him, the great, sweeping robes of midnight swallowed every step he left behind into a world of pitiless night.

The wind whipped through Charidor's hair as he pounded the leaf litter, his eyes peeled for stray roots—or something worse—that hid among the leaves. In the hollow dark, an owl hooted, and Charidor's heightened ears caught the faintest whisper of wings. He fought to keep his eyes on the faithful beacon of light and the narrow path it created.

Pyr galloped valiantly at Charidor's heels, though unfortunately he still possessed enough breath to speak.

"Of all the hideous, gnashing creatures—" he huffed. "Of all the tooth-grinning jaguars, all the slinking serpents, poison-tipped lizards and"—*huff, huff*—"trap-spinning spiders creeping in the shadows of this monstrous forest, why (oh! Why?) do we have to be running after wolves? Why couldn't it have been"—*huff, huff*—"flesh-eating bats? I mean, sure, they swoop on you out of nowhere and have a hundred teeth like tiny knives, but at least they're better than *wolves*!"

Charidor was only half listening, or rather, trying not to listen to the rest of Pyr's Encyclopedia of Forest Carnivores Ready to Eat You Any Moment Now.

The other half of his mind wandered up above the tree line. Any Star in full glow could easily glide up there, stepping on light air in great, unhindered leaps, fearlessly blazing across the night sky to the boy's rescue.

A root clamped itself over Charidor's bare foot, and his cheek suddenly hit the dirt. The sharp, bitter taste of earth coated his tongue.

"Charidor!" Pyr shouted, cutting short his litany on the differences between wolves and piranhas.

The young Star groped in the dust for the lantern. His palm hit warm metal.

"I'm fine." He let out the breath he was holding.

He climbed to his feet, brushing the dirt from his robes. "But, Pyr—"

"Hmm?" The glowing blue fox was all points and wide eyes.

"Maybe we can give the Flesh-Eating Monster list a rest for now?"

Pyr ducked his head. "Sorry."

Charidor gave him a grin. "Come on. Let's keep moving."

They pounded along the gleaming path, but after only a few strides, the lantern's fire washed out into a small, rocky clearing. Scattered boulders clambered their way up the hillside to a gaping maw of darkness.

The young Star's long strides fell to a halt. "This is the cave."

As the words left his lips, a howl pierced the night at his back.

Charidor whirled.

The lantern's golden beam barely rimmed the top of the empty hills.

He tensed, planting his feet into a firm stance.

Beside him, Pyr hunched his shoulders, eyeing off the shadows.

"We'll be all right," Charidor told him, gripping the lantern hard. "As long as we stay in the light."

Pyr raised his head and straightened his back. "I won't let you face them alone." But tension gripped his words.

Thin, clawlike tree limbs rattled over the clearing. Icy air from the cave's gaping mouth breathed at his neck. Beyond the lantern's circle, the empty stare of night kept watch, as if to guard over its secrets.

Two cold, yellow eyes glinted in the dark.

From atop the hill, a sleek, dark-grey wolf strode into the light. It lifted a proud head and howled into the wind.

Two more grey shadows prowled over the crest and into the lantern's gaze.

Pyr ducked his chin low, turning his head between each beast, but his paws dug into the hard dirt.

"Don't worry," Charidor said. "I'll have your back."

The fox steadied his gaze with a low growl. "And I'll have yours."

The hulking wolf leader paced over the jagged slabs of rock, baring its teeth. Its snarling companions slunk into its slipstream, sharp ears pointed behind them.

Charidor held a breath, clenching his empty fist.

The boy's only chance at survival relied solely on a fox, a glowless Star, and the tiny light in Charidor's hand.

Yes, a misty whisper chittered by his ear. *Such a little thing stands between the sweeping ocean of night and its prey.*

He shuddered.

Focus, Charidor!

The wolf leader pounced.

Its teeth dove at his face.

His swift strike shot through the night, catching the wolf on the shoulder.

It yelped and tumbled onto a pile of stones.

Beside him, a streak of blue flashed and collided with another wolf, who snapped its jaws.

A third wolf lunged at Charidor. He ducked, and a cold lash of air whipped by his head.

The wolf landed a few feet away, and Charidor whirled to face it.

In the corner of his eye, Pyr's wolf yelped and staggered. Charidor's wolf edged closer, its teeth flashing a malignant yellow against the lantern's amber beam.

A second wet snarl rumbled at his back, and he sidestepped to find the alpha wolf creeping up on him. The two wolves slowly backed Charidor to the silent cave entrance. An icy, boned hand slithered along his shoulders.

He drove a bare foot into the dust.

The alpha wolf lunged.

Charidor dodged to the side, but the edge of its bite caught skin, and steel daggers sliced into his arm. He yelled, but quick as light, he threw a fist, catching the wolf's hindquarters. It lost footing as it hit the dirt and rolled away.

A second grey streak flashed toward him.

Charidor awkwardly swung the lantern out of the way, but the hard steel hit his kneecap. He winced, yet with a shooting sweep of his hand, he swung at the wolf's shoulders, catching fur and following with a kick swift as starlight.

The wolf tumbled. It scrambled to its paws and yelped away into the night.

Charidor straightened and thrust his lantern at the retreating shadow. Maybe he could hold a defense against the night after all.

"Charidor, watch out!"

He turned. An arrow of steel-grey fur soared toward him, wild yellow eyes and teeth a mere arms-reach from Charidor's neck.

He couldn't blink. He couldn't move.

A lightning bolt of blue and green blazed to the steel torpedo's side. Pyr struck and both wolf and fox veered a hairsbreadth from Charidor's head. The wolf's leg clipped the lantern, launching it from his grasp with a sickening crack.

The shadows rushed in.

Charidor darted for the lantern. It had smashed into pieces over a thick, fallen branch. The wind's fingers played with the flame, which threw sputtering orange spotlights around the clearing. He picked through the gleaming shards of glass, hissing as the hot, gasping flame bit his fingertips.

Three shrill yelps pierced the quiet.

Pyr!

Charidor grabbed the thick branch under the lantern. Its dry leaves caught the dying flame and roared to life in a billow of black smoke. The blazing branch threw its light over a grey mass of muscle and fur as it wrestled with a struggling blue glow.

With a mighty roar, Charidor swung wide the burning branch.

The alpha wolf spun from its prey and eyed the flame. It staggered back a step.

Charidor whipped his new weapon side to side, shouting wildly into the wind.

The dancing flames whooshed a whisker from the predator's face and the alpha wolf turned and fled into the moonless night like a shadow from the sun.

Its remaining companion streaked after it, howling, until both had vanished into the waiting dark.

Charidor flew to Pyr's side, flinging down the branch. Already, its leaves had crumpled, and smoke and flame had died down to a flickering ember.

The fox's own aurora glow, too, had faded.

Dark blood oozed from his shoulder.

"Oh, Pyr!" Charidor tore a ribbon of cloth from his nightrobes and daubed the lacerated skin. Blood-soaked green fur, soft as new wheat, clumped in sticky patches. Pyr must have defended valiantly, because the wolf's bite had not cut deep.

Charidor gritted his teeth. "I told you I'd have your back."

Cold shadows licked at his heels between dying gasps of light. He squeezed his eyes shut. "Why am I so afraid of it? Why do I always run? I'll never be strong enough to face the dark." Shuddering, he opened his eyes and ripped free another piece of cloth. "How can I even call myself a Star?"

Gently, he wound the cloth around his friend's shoulder.

"No. You faced the dark." Pyr's soft voice cracked in the cold. "You saved me."

Charidor carefully tied off the bandage. "That wolf never should've gotten to you."

Pyr shivered, and the young Star scanned the dim clearing for shelter. Beneath the roiling, unbroken cloak of clouds, the lantern flame still clung to its wick in the dust as if warbling its low, orange swan song into the night. It wouldn't last much longer.

Soon, the dark would come.

The wind hurled through the valley, and the tiny flame flared in a wild gasp of light. It threw a shaky orange hand over the hills. As it fell away, a little alcove nestled in the highest boulders drank up the fading glow.

Shadows covered the hill once more.

Fighting to keep his focus on his friend, Charidor gently lifted the fox, cradling the warm but shivering animal to his chest, and Pyr buried his nose into his shirt.

Charidor climbed up the hill and, with the fox's soft fur brushing his arm, lifted Pyr up into the alcove. At least, up so high, he should be safe enough from danger.

The fox curled his nose into the bed of stray leaves. A weak blue-green haze lit the corners of the small alcove as he glanced up at Charidor.

"Go," he murmured. "The boy needs you. You're his only light, now."

A chilled breath from the cave bristled along Charidor's neck. He hunched his shoulders. "I won't be able to see a thing down there."

"You're a Star, aren't you?" came the weak reply. "Use your ears."

Charidor closed his eyes, drawing in a deep breath.

For aeons, Stars had responded to the Calls of all who cried out in the dark. But now, only he stood in reach of this boy lost in the shadows.

Could he be a Star tonight?

"Go, before another creature comes for him."

Charidor clenched his fists and stepped down from the alcove. "Stay safe, Pyr." He turned to face the cave.

The narrow opening of darkness beckoned like a hungry, hollow eye, watching him behind creeping ashen mist, as if waiting to drag him from the light.

Steeling himself, he stepped through the wild grass until only the cave's black throat gaped before him.

Shivering, he turned back.

A tiny flame still struggled in the clearing. He couldn't leave it.

A musty wind from the cave hovered over the sweat beading on his arm and lingered as though it were a figure that stood behind his shoulder. It blew a quick, strong breath.

The flame winked out.

Long, snaking tendrils of shadow slithered from every crevice of the cave. Quiet scuttling pattered near his feet and scurried away into whatever deep lairs lay hidden in the darkness. Stretching out a groping palm, Charidor plunged another bare foot into the cold, endless shadow.

A bat screeched as it flew by his right ear.

He sucked in a sharp breath.

"Peace, Charidor." He let out a sigh. "You're the only Star the boy has. Use your ears."

The bat's flapping faded into the darkness.

He tilted his head, listening far into the corridors of the cave.

A distant, faint echo lapped against his ear.

Gathering his strength, Charidor strode toward the boy's voice.

Or did the echo belong to the bat?

A cool prickle like icy fingertips crept over his skin.

He scowled, shaking cold and doubt from his mind. He pushed ahead into the dark and toward the dim voice.

As he walked, the shadows hunched in their shoulders, peering closely at him before stepping back to loom high over the path.

Straight ahead, a thick shadow watched him. Its eyes, hungry and intense, gleamed wider with every step he took.

A breath away from the dark figure's face, Charidor stopped.

Struggling to inhale enough fresh air, he lifted a chin to the shadow.

Come, Charidor. It's only the dark.

He raised a foot... and ploughed his shin into a sharp rock.

Crying out, he clutched his leg and bounced in circles until...

He froze.

Which way was the boy's echo?

He shut his eyes, straining to listen.

He turned left, then right, and then—

There! A whisper, far off in the cave. Was it the boy?

He stepped toward it...

And tumbled into empty space.

His shoulder struck a knuckle of stone, and he rolled, end over end over jagged bones of rock, tumbling faster, until his body slammed into hard clay.

He groaned.

Musty, damp air slipped like thick fingers down his throat.

Coughing, he wrestled onto his back, trying to pull in a clear breath.

High above, a soaring cathedral of pitch darkness stared down at him without mercy.

Something like a cold, shadowy chin leaned over his shoulder. *Funny. Ever heard of a Star lost in the dark? Hmm, I wonder if it'll ever find its way out again.*

Charidor gasped for air, fighting to his feet against the sting of a dozen sharp cuts and countless bruises.

The ground shifted, and he slipped. His cheek landed in thick mud. His nostrils filled with the stale, sickly-sweet scent of something rotting.

Like a grave.

He yelled, blood pounding in his ears. He threw himself forward, slipping, groping over dirt, over mud, until his hands hit a slope of dry rocks. He climbed, desperate to escape the ravenous, slimy jaws of this monstrous cave!

Above him, like a miracle, a little gush of moonlight opened like a tiny doorway.

A guttural cry caught in his throat.

He threw himself, hands and toes, toward the moonlight. He wasn't made to be in the dark!

The ground shuddered and a stone slipped beneath his heel.

He fell.

His elbow cracked on rock, and he tumbled, stones breaking loose beneath him.

His jaw hit the spiked stone floor. Stillness settled over the cave.

A numbing tingle slowly crept over his leg.

He felt for damage to his body, but his fingers touched hard rock.

No!

He shoved and prodded, but his numb leg had been completely encased by stone.

His forehead fell into the dust.

The cave had buried him in the pit of the earth.

"I thought I could do something to help," he whispered. "But who am I fooling? I am no Star."

Somewhere in the distance, a shimmering light swam like a drop of silver fire at the bottom of a well.

"Father?"

A warm touch of starlight brushed his cheek. A memory stirred, and he was a child once more...

Charidor shivered, hugging his father's robe tight around his wet shoulders. "I never want to go near another well again."

A few hours earlier, he'd tried to rescue a little bird caught in some string, and he slipped and fell into the village well. He landed headfirst with a stinging splash. The shadows crept closer to him, and he cried out for help. A silver light instantly shot through the sky and his father's brilliant glow filled the world above the well.

Now he sat beside his father on the mountain's edge, watching as the last pale fingers of twilight slipped below the sleepy village. Above them, the first gleaming gemstones of the night began to string together their silver Constellations over a cloudless sky.

"Father, what is it like up there?"

The Evening Star hummed a low, musing note. "It's quite lonely at times. Though, peaceful too, watching a sleeping planet from a distance."

The Stars sparkled brighter, like seashells in a rockpool suddenly caressed by sunlight.

"Yet, it always requires something of you." His father leaned forward, resting his chin between glowing fingers. "Every evening, you leave home and comfort and climb into the deepest reaches of space. Some nights, the darkness is so thick you think your light will never make it through. Yet still you shine, in the hope that your strongest glow might break open a tiny corner of the night sky. And just maybe, that small light in the sky will be enough to guide a weary traveler back home to their family."

In the distance, two birds, hardly more than faint blue specks, rose and twirled among the last of the light.

Charidor huddled deeper into his father's robe. "I don't know if I can shine that bright."

A strong hand clasped his shoulder. He met his father's fiery gaze, blazing with the limitless wonder of a hundred galaxies. "Charidor, listen to me. It doesn't matter how bright your light is. But to push against the dark with everything inside you, whether or not your light ever breaks through, that's what it means to be a Star."

The memory faded. Charidor reached his chin to the sky, but his father had vanished, swallowed by shadow.

His shoulders sank to the stones. He shivered.

Somewhere in the ocean depths of darkness, perhaps the boy, too, shivered, lost overboard to the night, huddled alone so far from home and family.

Yet he could do nothing in the dark but stare.

Some nights, the darkness is so thick you think your light will never make it through.

"Father. I have no light to give."

A fiery gaze flashed over the shadows. *But to push against the dark with everything inside you, that's what it means to be a Star.*

Charidor clenched his teeth.

Despair weighed down his bones like a mountain.

And yet...

What if he did have something left inside him? What if a tiny shred of strength still lingered?

One little shove against the dark.

He tightened a fist.

Surely, the boy deserved that much.

Sucking in the deep, cold air, he heaved his weight against the stone nearly crushing his leg. But he fell to the dust, rasping for breath, the stone unmoved.

Push! With everything inside you!

He let out a moan, low and grating, and shoved his whole body against the rocks. Groaning, straining, his muscles trembled. He clamped his jaw and leaned against the rocks and the mountain. Against the cave and against the shadows that always mocked him in the night.

With a mighty roar, the stone shifted, and he rose against a tumbling clatter of rocks.

He stood to his full height.

Red heat sparked in his chest.

He lifted his brow to the sky. "Thank you, Father."

"Please. Is somebody there?"

The echo of the boy's Call rippled out from a chamber not far from where Charidor stood.

His heart pounded.

He had fallen so close to the boy!

He squared his shoulders. The time had come to be a Warrior in the night, whether or not his Light ever appeared.

Something flickered in the shadows. He leaned forward, squinting. A low, murky opening flittered between the rocks.

He crawled over stones, crouched beneath the opening, and he climbed up into a wide chamber. A hole in the roof reunited him with the night sky.

Pale moonlight shone through a thinning veil of clouds and shimmered down the smooth cave walls as if painted by soft fingers. In the chamber's farthest corner, a tangle of forest vines crawled over the rocks.

Charidor crept over moss and gnarled roots, following the echo to an old, dark well that had been cut into the stone floor. The abandoned well swirled with shadow, a churning, angry darkness.

He swallowed back the urge to flee.

The boy's Call pulsed toward him. As he listened, he pinched onto the source of the sound, but it lay far deeper in the well than he could reach.

Any glowing Star would simply leap into the well and glide down on starlit steps.

He blew a steady breath.

Would he let the dark win when the boy lay so near?

Beside him, a faint coat of milky light shimmered like water over the wall of vines.

Vines!

"Hold on, down there. I'm coming!"

Charidor pulled at the thick, green web beside him, tearing off long cords of vine. He tied them end to end until a great, trailing rope coiled around the moonlit cave. He tugged the rope tight around a knuckle of stone and dragged it to the black well.

He edged his bare toes over the rim.

The shadows peered at him, whispering, widening into deep, leering grins.

Charidor squeezed his eyes shut. Sight had no more use for him now.

A moist, sickly-sweet wind pushed a warm, stale breath over his face. *You will not come back up again...*

He clamped his jaw and took a soft step into nothing.

Musty breeze whipped through his hair and nightrobes. Shadows hissed by his cheeks.

The vine-rope pulled taut.

His toes slammed against a mossy brick wall. Taking in the damp, earthy air, he edged down the rope, tracing a path over the bricks and misshapen tree roots.

Wet stone nudged his shoulder.

As his closed eyes began to relax, he became aware of something else.

Something lingering a hands-reach away.

Like little, bright fingers tickling his eyelids.

He fluttered them open.

A soft ring of silver light brushed along the edges of the old, mossy bricks, wrapping around him in a gleaming circle.

He stared.

Darkness gaped above him. Shadows below. Yet still the glowing circle rippled its gentle silver smile.

How...?

A shout rang from below.

The soft fingers of pearlescent light touched the face of a boy beneath him, his straw-colored hair caked in mud. Yet underneath his blackened eyes, a wide grin beamed like morning.

"You're glowing!" the boy cried.

Charidor shimmied down the vine, a dizzy tingle swirling in his head, and stretched his feet into the thick pile of leaves coating the pit floor. A silver gleam lined each stem and leaf. Everything around him, moss, ferns, the ragged boy staring up at him with huge eyes, clothed in... starlight?

His starlight.

Impossible...

"Are you a Star?" the little boy squeaked. He cradled his scratched and bloodied arms against his shivering body. His overalls had torn in several places. A blue-and-black bruise marred his cheek. He needed warmth. And food. But first, he needed to be rescued from this pit.

Tilting his head, Charidor lifted a silver foot into the air, as though stepping up an invisible staircase.

His toes touched something firm yet smooth as warm silk, and the pale diamond glow brightened. Tingling thrills of light shot through his entire body.

He turned to the boy. "Yes," he said, his words running warm ripples through his lungs. "I am a Star." He held out a hand. "And it's time I brought you home."

The boy ran and clutched Charidor's side.

The young Star stepped another foot up the impossible staircase.

Again, it touched silk, and again the silver shine strengthened. Up and up he stepped, and as they rose through the dark pit, a deep, radiating warmth burst from the innermost chambers of his heart, pushing great, silver fingers through the shadows.

As they stepped over the well, and higher, above the cave roof, his miraculous glow spread triumphant hands up to a sky that had cleared into a thousand glitters. The light streamed out its clear, silver song, shouting, dancing – leaping! – over mountaintops. And all the while, the echo of four impossible, yet glorious words beamed out to his shining kin:

"I am a Star!"

The next evening, the whole town gathered under the shining, golden pillars of Skykeeper Promenade, all abuzz to see a new Star take up his Assignment.

Catching two familiar faces in the crowd, Charidor sprinted down the hillside in a silver blur to meet Pyr and the boy, Runi, both covered in an army of bandages.

Charidor ruffled Runi's straw-colored hair. "Healer Minda finally let you both out of the infirmary, I see."

The boy giggled.

Pyr ducked his head, gazing up with golden eyes. His aurora coat once more cast a soft gleam onto the grass. "Why do you have to go all the way to Golark? Why choose an Assignment so far away?" His ears drooped. "There's not even another Star over that planet."

Charidor sighed, bending to rub the fox behind the ears. He'd pored over the assignment files for hours, but only one dazzled brighter than the rest as the afternoon sun drifted through the trees.

"That's why I have to go, Pyr. I can't bear the thought of even one more starless night over that dark planet." He rose in a soft wash of silver. "Besides, my light will only grow brighter and brighter still in the darkness. This my father assures me."

Pyr's whiskers and eyes glowed with all the pride of the grandest Aurora spectacle. "I always knew you had it in you."

Charidor couldn't help but smile. "Don't worry, pal. I'll come back soon to visit."

A strong hand fell on his shoulder, and his father's glow bathed them all in silver.

The Evening Star raised a mighty chin. "Come. Twilight is almost upon us."

Charidor followed his father to the deep green hillcrest above the Promenade. The sky over the forest had tilted its head into softening pink and orange clouds.

As the last rim of sunlight lingered at the world's edge, Charidor reached out, moving his fingers through the liquid-white glow that grew stronger with the fading dusk.

"It's strange," he said. "I used to think my Light would come when I wasn't watching. Maybe while I slept one night. I never expected I'd need to fight so hard to find it."

His father gazed beyond the horizon. "Nobody knows when a Star's Light will come. And yet, it always takes a trial." He turned to Charidor with quiet, burning eyes. His face softened, and he gave a brilliant smile that split the dark like a wide, dazzling horizon.

"I am proud of you, my son."

With that, his luminescent robes caught the night breeze, and the Evening Star took the first blazing step into the sky.

Still drinking in that dazzling horizon, Charidor breathed in deeply and raised a foot into the thinning dusk. It caught firm silk.

And, following his father, the son of the Evening Star climbed the invisible staircase of the sky until the villagers watching below could see only the smallest speck, shining in a dark corner of the night with a steady, silver gleam.

JAMES NOLLER

James Noller writes young adult novels from the fields of his Australian home, while his tiny dog longs to chase the kangaroos on the other side of the fence. Inspired to explore what "coming of age" means today, James creates fantasy stories to help teens face the challenges of growing up—without losing their wonder. Having written his first musical at age 16, James is an avid songwriter and often takes his storytelling to the stage in local theatre. Away from both page and stage, you'll likely find James plotting his revenge at *Catan* or inventing cheesy songs with his twin brother.

Achievements

- Completed four novels and a novella, and received multiple professional edit letters.

- Received manuscript requests from multiple publishers at the Realm Makers conference online.

- Hired as a fiction developmental editor and creative writing coach.

- Works as a marketing assistant for bestselling author Chuck Black, specializing in email marketing, podcast engineering, and copywriting.

- Worked as a podcast host for Story Embers, where he interviewed fiction authors on the finer points of story craft and theme.

- Operated a time management coaching business, which included designing and presenting the *Master Your Schedule for Writers* online masterclass, utilizing his skills of public speaking, email marketing, website design, and professional coaching.

- Holds a Bachelor of Arts (Creative Writing) from RMIT University.

Pitches

- A YA contemporary fantasy novel about an ignored teen girl who discovers that the new, most popular boy in town can rewind time and is using it to erase the mistakes of his perfect and ambitious family.

- *Percy Jackson* meets *Alex Rider* in a YA contemporary fantasy novel about a misfit Australian teen who "borrows" a high-tech boat, determined to rescue his missing mother from an island that shouldn't exist—until he discovers a hidden AI computer that reveals the double life his mother kept secret for years.

- A YA fantasy novella about a teenage boy doomed to teleport to another planet every time he touches another person—and how accidentally brushing a girl's hand sends them both on a journey from which only one of them can return.

Fantasy & Magical Realism
Adult

CAPTAIN OF THE MOONLIGHT

CALEB RENICH

"You're strong enough to lead them."

Captain Athareon had whispered those words as he affixed the epaulettes to Ulysses' shoulders with the crew watching at attention.

Then Athareon left.

Rumors of a Second Pirate Alliance had been brewing in the east across the Endless Ocean, and the Crown Prince of Theion required his most trusted mediator and war hero. Athareon answered the summons, leaving his ship, his beloved crew, a hold filled with medicine worth its weight in gold, and a newly minted Captain Ulysses behind.

For two days, Ulysses had believed those words.

The crew's songs had been loud and merry, their salutes crisp, and *Moonlight*–a beautiful three-masted frigate–danced from wave to wave like a bride on her wedding day. The work had hardly been laborious at all, and even the sun and wind seemed to laugh during those two beautiful days.

Then the fog came.

A suffocating wall of swirling, dark mist that drained the color and life from every surface. Ulysses had watched it from this very place, standing at the prow like a dragon guarding its clutch.

Captain Athareon had sailed them through fog banks before, and at first, Ulysses thought he could, too, even after the smiling sunshine disappeared, and they sailed into the darkening mists.

Now, the dance became a slog.

Ulysses stood on the prow, robbed of his draconic illusions of grandeur and staring at endless nothing.

Nine days. Nine days without sunlight.

Something broke in Ulysses to admit it. *I miss the light.*

Footsteps startled Ulysses from his reverie. Manaris approached with a welcome smile, defiant against the oppressive grey.

"Report?" Ulysses asked.

"All's well, Ulysses, sir. The men are tired, but it's nearly second bell, and I convinced Kavros we could spare one day of generous rations to boost morale. Two small fights. Kavros has been stirring up the greenies against our crew, but I sorted them before it got ugly. We should see Port Tyr within the next two days, by Ven's reckoning."

"Good." Ulysses tried not to feel dwarfed by Manaris' lanky height. *Caela should be off watch soon. I should check on her and make sure she's all right.* "And the hold?"

"Glowing as steady as ever."

"Good," Ulysses said, breathing a sigh of relief.

The wraithleaf in the hold was the only substance known to cure hag's plague, and they were carrying enough for two islands of Tyr's size. Assuming they reached harbor safely. Wraithleaf's otherworldly healing properties were a question for alchemists and arcanists, but Ulysses did know that the slightest change in temperature or pressure, and the ghostly-glowing leaf would snuff out and lose its healing properties.

Manaris lingered, face pleasant but feet planted at attention. Manaris stared him down until Ulysses caved and shifted his eyes to his boots.

Blight that man and whoever taught him to read me. "The hirelings"—Ulysses calling them green felt hypocritical—"are saying we should have reached Port Tyr a day ago."

Manaris shrugged. "The winds have been strange, and we've lost time around the rocks off Kieros. If we hold true to Athareon's course, we'll come through." He winked and ambled away.

Just hold true. Just be like Athareon. Ulysses' hands begin to shake. Clenching them could only slow the mounting tension in his chest.

Something escaped him, like a mast splintering under heavy wind, and he blurted, "What would you do if Athareon had picked you?"

Manaris stopped and turned. "Come again, Uly? Er, sir."

Ulysses' cheeks burned. *What kind of a question was that?* The crew already grumbled that the ship was cursed and they would all die at sea. What would happen if their captain began spewing his doubts like a greenie who hadn't found his sea legs?

"I said, 'What do you think about checking our speed once more?' Ven always likes the most accurate measurements."

Manaris wrinkled his brow but nodded. "Of course."

Ulysses shuddered and turned back towards the shrouded sea, listening to the rhythmic crashing of invisible waves. Maybe if he had just a little light, he wouldn't ask foolish questions or brood on the prow. He could be like Athareon. Athareon didn't make mistakes.

Except, of course, when he made me captain. Ulysses thought. *I suppose there is a first time for everything.*

Muffled voices sneaking through the fog made his spine stiffen.

Wonderful, he scoffed to himself, *now I'm hearing things.* But when he turned, two figures–Caela and Delcanis–scuttled down the rigging from the crow's nest, swiping at one another and shouting. A growing crowd beneath called out warnings and caution. *Second bell! They're changing watch.*

He hurried off the fo'c'sle and joined the crowd as the pair of lookouts reached the deck, yelling at one another in pitched voices. He tried to press through the bodies, but he couldn't muscle through until Manaris cried, "Oi! Attention!"

The human wall parted, and the crew hushed, save for Caela and Delcanis wrestling on the dew-slick deck over a spyglass.

Before Ulysses could get a word out, Caela gripped the spyglass with both hands and planted a kick in Delcanis' gut. He groaned as Caela spun away.

"Liar!" she shrieked, as she crawled away and snatched up her battered tricorn hat. "I didn't see a thing all night. You could get us all killed if you run your mouth to get attention!"

"That's *rich* coming from the spoiled brat stowaway!" Delcanis, a few years her senior, wiped sweat from his ruddy brow and sprang to his feet. "You don't know a blighted thing about the sea. I've spent my life here, and I know what I saw!"

Caela righted herself, glanced around, and seemed to wilt from the weight of the eyes on her.

Ulysses stepped between them. "Calm yourselves. What did you see?"

Delcanis stared at Ulysses, the veins in his neck throbbing, which added to the electricity in the air.

"Land," Caela whispered, "He said he saw land."

Murmurs rippled through the crew. *Land?* Ven, who had just emerged from her quarters with her dark robes creased and rumpled from hunching over maps, was the best chartmaster in the Sea of Theion, but that didn't stop the thoughts gnawing at his mind. *Could we have missed Tyr entirely?*

All eyes turned on Ulysses.

Caela hugged the spyglass to her chest and edged behind him.

If only Ulysses could hide behind someone, too.

A sea of faces surrounded him, and he drowned in their gazes. Familiar faces like Manaris and Ven nodded encouragingly. But others glowered. Hirelings from Akar who got more than they bargained for, green naval recruits with eyes like cornered animals, and then Kavros, like a great serpent lurking beneath the waves.

What would Athareon say? "It's..." Ulysses puffed up his chest and made level eye contact with his crew. *His* crew, he reminded himself. "The people of Tyr are dying. If there's the slightest chance we could save them, we must stay the course."

No voice rose to challenge him.

Maybe I can do this.

The tap-shuffle of Kavros' limp sounded behind him, and Ulysses felt his sails deflate. Kavros' body twisted as he walked, but the old injury gave his silhouette a predatory edge.

Kavros hadn't been recruited, but assigned to the *Moonlight* by the High Admiral of Theion for his decorated tenure. Ulysses had been unable to refuse an honored war veteran, however distasteful his personality. Sailors parted around him as he limped up to Ulysses. "A fine speech," he growled. "Same as the one my commander gave during the Skerion Conflict, right before he led my company straight into a cavalry charge."

Ulysses bristled but found himself tongue-tied.

"Noble words from a noble man. Any of you fine fellows feeling noble today? We have three days of spare rations before I vote to toss the useless overboard as bait for the sea snakes, and I don't fancy spending those three days chasing an island that *might* be behind the next wave."

The hirelings grumbled their assent, and Ulysses felt his authority vanish like moonbeams swallowed by the fog.

"Hold your tongue, before I fork it to match the rest of you!"

Ulysses flinched at Ven's sharp voice as she stepped into the fray.

"I know our course, and we've yet to reach Tyr. If we stray now, noble or otherwise, we'll run aground and breathe seawater before the day is out."

"Oi, forget Tyr! I've got a family!" hollered a sailor.

"Easy now, let's talk about this. Captain left us a mission. We can't abandon it!" Manaris stepped into the breach and sent Ulysses a pleading look. "Come on, Uly."

"Speak up, *Captain*," spat Kavros.

Something dark twisted inside Ulysses' mind.

Athareon could wave his hand, and the crew would snap to attention. He spoke like he could see the future, as if the winds would bend to his will.

Captain Athareon is probably negotiating peace with the Pirate Alliance right now, and here I am stuck in a fog bank on my first voyage. He made me a captain. I had better act like one.

"Quiet!" Ulysses shouted.

Caela flinched at his tone, but the chatter stilled. In the silence, Ulysses realized he hadn't the faintest clue what he had decided. He looked at Manaris, then at Kavros. Manaris would listen, even if he disagreed. But if Ulysses didn't placate Kavros, the rest of the crew would mutiny. "We make for the land. Delcanis, give your best reckoning to Ven. Inform helmsman Skander of our change in course."

Delcanis puffed out his chest, Ven gaped, and Kavros smiled smugly.

Ulysses swallowed the burning lump of shame in his throat and began ordering the crew, whilst trying to avoid Manaris' gaze. *The medicine has to make it to Tyr. If the crew can't hold together, there won't be a ship to get it there.*

Ulysses stood on the quarterdeck when Ven marched up to him, her grey robes trailing like a veil of storm clouds.

She jabbed a finger into his chest. "Oi! Why did you choose *him* over *us*?"

"I'm sorry—"

"Aye, I'm sorry, too! That fool boy doesn't know a thing about reckoning, and it's going to get us all killed."

"Ven, please. Did he give you a heading that you can trust?"

"As good a heading as a drunken sea slug could give, but aye, he did... And, well, it *could* work. But we're too close to turn back! I haven't got time to sound and make sure we don't run aground. This is dangerous, Ulysses. Sir."

"Could it be true?" Ulysses leaned in to whisper, "Could he really have seen land?"

Ven's eyes narrowed, "Are you *really* asking me this?"

Ulysses gritted his teeth. He saw Kavros watching from the corner of his eye. "Can we make it?"

"We—" She looked down. "We could, aye. But water depth would be a concern. I could sound for more accurate readings, but even then my reckoning could be off..."

Slowing to take measurements will only rile Kavros and his gang. An unwelcome shiver tickled his spine. "We make for Delcanis' heading. It's a risk, but one we'll have to take. Can you work with Skander to navigate us through?"

Ven worked her jaw slowly, then nodded, her robes swishing behind her as she joined the mountainous helmsman.

Skander called a greeting in his country's language, giving a salute so enthusiastic that his Irin dragonscale armor clattered.

"Sir?" A small voice piped from behind him. "Why did you choose Delcanis over me?"

"I'm sorry?" Ulysses turned and almost tripped over Caela, her battered tricorn right under his nose.

"Forgive me, Captain." Her lilting accent grew thicker as she continued, "I don't mean to question your leadership—believe me, that's the last thing I want. But I just... I want to know why you chose how you did."

Ulysses crouched to meet her eyes under the brim of her hat. "Oh, Caela, I'm sorry about all that. I do trust you. But sailors sometimes need convincing before they offer their trust. Sometimes you have to make compromises, or... be creative." He nodded subtly at her shiny leather boots, once Delcanis' pride and joy. She had won them with a suspicious turn of good luck at the dice table, orchestrated by Ulysses with discreet signals behind Delcanis' back, thus earning herself a position on the watch.

A slow smile spread across her face. "I understand, sir. I don't know much about captains, but you must be one of the good ones."

Ulysses straightened in his captain's uniform as she ducked away towards the crew quarters.

His momentary confidence faltered as his eyes shifted to the deck. Athareon's old crew and the hirelings circled each other like gladiators as they worked. Their glares flew with enough force to nearly whip up the fog into a proper storm. They still sang to keep rhythm, of course, but each verse held a desperate edge. The fog soon swallowed their voices, and Ulysses sensed the crew sang not for joy, but to keep the beast fed lest it decide to take them.

I just need to find land and let the fog pass. A little light, and they'll come around.

Manaris met Ulysses on the quarterdeck less than a turn of the glass later, and the pair watched the scurrying of seamen.

"Report?" Ulysses asked.

"All's well, Ulysses," he replied. "The ship is on her new heading, and Kavros and his men are satisfied. For now."

"Manaris, I—"

"Please, don't apologize. You're the captain, aren't you? You make the decision you feel is best, and I make it happen."

Ulysses bit his lip. Manaris wasn't smiling anymore. But as Ulysses opened his mouth to speak, the deck lurched under the force of a large wave.

No, not a wave.

The hull groaned, like the dying cry of a great sea serpent.

Men staggered. Crates slid toward the edge of the deck and threatened to plunge overboard, and the mast creaked as wind pulled it forward against the will of the deck.

We've run aground!

Ulysses' eyes raced across the ship. He could almost hear Athareon's voice in his ear as his instincts assembled pieces of the puzzle. The wind had been favorable, but now, the cloth sails strained at the rigging and forced the hull further into the ground—sand or mud, he concluded, not stone.

Without quick action, they would sink or be stranded. Another groan from the hull, louder this time. *Moonlight* was too heavy, even without the weight of the already-consumed rations, and they needed to change their tack to steer out of the sandbar.

"Heave to!" Ulysses bellowed to the stunned crewmen and women. He cried again, "We've run aground! Heave to!"

The crew exploded into motion.

"We need to jettison the ballast, and maybe some supplies," Ulysses called to Manaris as he dashed to the steps off the quarterdeck. "I'll organize—"

"Wait." A hand gripped his shoulder, and Ulysses whirled around into the piercing gaze of his first mate. "Sir. Kavros knows the hold better than any, and his men will obey him. *Moonlight* needs her captain."

Ulysses saw no shadow of Manaris' hurt. The crew's safety was bigger than any petty squabble. And blighted moons, if Manaris wasn't *right*. Ulysses swallowed the knot of fear and took a grateful breath. *Bless that man and whoever*

"I said it's my turn. Respectfully, sir, it's my fault we're in this mess. Please let me help."

"You can relieve him." Ulysses nodded towards the other sailor. "I'm not leaving."

"Captain, that's no way to talk," said the second voice, sweet and lightly accented. "And besides that, I need to talk with you." *Caela.*

Ulysses stepped away from the bilge pump, and Delcanis took his place.

Caela gripped Ulysses' hand and led him deeper into the hold. She sat him down on a crate and then fidgeted with the hem of her long tunic. "I brought you something, sir, but you can't tell Mr. Kavros. Please?" She produced a steaming cup of tea, complete with a dainty teacup and saucer. "Delcanis swore I couldn't swipe something out from Mr. Kavros' stores, but I did, and then I got scared he'd tar and feather me if he found out. But when I saw you down here, well, I used to make Father tea when he was upset, and—"

"It's perfect," Ulysses smiled, accepting the cup. "Thank you."

Caela sat down opposite Ulysses and watched intently until he took a sip. The warmth seared his lips at first, but the sweet, floral taste flooded onto his tongue and fought back against the clouds in his mind. He shivered, realizing he was freezing.

"What are we going to do, Captain?" Caela asked.

Ulysses flinched at the whispers in the mist again. "You don't have to call me that."

Caela furrowed her brow. "But you are the captain, aren't you?"

"Not like Athareon."

A long silence.

"What... what was he like? I only knew him for a short while, and most of that time I spent hoping he wouldn't notice me. But you speak so highly of him. He must have been a great man."

"Athareon always knew what to do. He sailed these seas for more than a decade during the Pirate Alliance Wars. Crown Prince Aryth even offered him an admiral position leading a fleet. A fleet! But he chose to deliver medicine, search for survivors of shipwrecks, or... mentor a boy from a no-name town who wanted to sail. He's the best of the best.

"But me?" Ulysses huffed, feeling like a child before this fourteen-year-old stowaway, "I have nothing. I'm a fake. Athareon knew how to *lead*. Every order he gave turned out to be exactly the right thing to do, and... he would still find time to speak with me and listen to what I had to say. Actually, just like–" Ulysses' voice caught in his throat, the warmth of the tea making his fingers prickle.

"Sir?"

"Actually, just like what you're doing right now."

"Really?" Caela laughed. "But I don't know anything about helping people. I'm copying you!"

Ulysses raised an eyebrow.

"When Kavros first found me down here, I was right scared. None of the other crew would talk to me. I couldn't tie a knot or hoist sails or... anything. I thought you all would ship me back to Karth and Father the first chance you could. But *you* sat with me. You asked me questions and made me feel like a person again. Helped me"—she paused, nodding towards the shiny leather boots now half submerged in seawater—"earn the respect of the crew."

Ulysses grinned at that.

"You listened to me. I don't know if that makes you a good captain, but it does make you a good person. Maybe that's what your captain saw in you."

Ulysses finished his tea. Something like sunlight seemed to push back against the darkness around him. He no longer felt the cold. "I think... Maybe you're right, Caela. Thank you. You know, one day you might make a fine captain yourself."

"Oh, heavens." Her eyes bulged, and she laughed nervously. "Please, no thank you."

Ulysses took a breath and stood. His captain's uniform was somewhere beneath a foot of seawater, so he left it. He rolled up the sleeves of his thin white tunic and climbed the ladder to the deck. When he emerged, Caela in tow behind him, the oppressive closeness of the fog surrounded him again. It clung tightly to the deck and wreathed the sails and rigging.

Ulysses pushed back against it.

The crew milled about on deck, some slouched against the rail, some wandered listlessly, and others argued in small pockets. At least they had tacked the sails to keep them from moving too quickly, the wind keeping tension between the two differently-angled sails. Under pressure but going nowhere. Ulysses found Kavros and Manaris shouting on the quarterdeck. Skander leaned lazily against the wheel, and Ven stood behind them all, staring out into the fog and muttering to herself.

"Kavros! Manaris! With me."

Both men froze, Kavros' finger stabbing Manaris' chest, whose arms were brandished like clubs. They took Ulysses in from top to bottom before they lowered their hands and followed.

Ulysses stood by the rail with his back to the fog and spoke. "What is this all about?"

"This man!" Manaris huffed, his face red. "This man misleads you, manipulates our crew, and then has the audacity to blame me for–for–gah!"

"If it's anyone's fault, it's that fool boy finding shapes in the mist! I take no responsibility for—"

"No," Ulysses said. "The fault is mine. The captain makes the decision, so the captain bears the fault. Everyone on this ship trusted Captain Athareon, so I tried to become him."

"But Uly, sir," Manaris interjected with a glare at Kavros, "the crew is supposed to trust their captain!"

Ulysses laughed. "And a captain should never ask his crew to do something he wouldn't do himself. That was my mistake. No more of that. I'm sorry."

"That's lovely," Kavros growled, "but last I checked, we're short on rations without a heading. When the men are starving and ready to mutiny, are you going to give them a cute speech, too?"

"What would you have us do?"

"Well, throw Grift overboard, for starters, he always leaves his—"

Ulysses held out a hand. "No. Honestly. What do *you* think we should do?"

Kavros opened his mouth as if to retort and—a welcome surprise—shut it again. "I don't want to spend a minute more in this fog if I don't have to. I say we scour the charts and find some safe haven and cower like dogs till this passes. But in the meantime, we're low on rations. Tyr or the moon's own backside, we won't make it anywhere if we don't take inventory."

"Manaris?"

"The men... are scared. Blighted moons, captain, *I'm* scared. Men don't think straight in this kind of darkness. They don't need rules and order; they need to know that somebody will watch over them."

Ulysses nodded. "Ven?"

Ven stared into the fog, the wind rustling her robe. "Please... no. If I had kept better track of our heading, we wouldn't have... Best if you ask somebody else."

Ulysses put his hand on her shoulder and turned her away from the mist. "Ven. Look at me. You were right about Tyr from the beginning. I'm the one to blame for this, not you. We can go over the ship's log again or work out your reckoning on the charts." Ulysses forced a chuckle. "I would even make the whole crew study nautical history with you if it would help."

Ven's spine straightened.

"What?" Ulysses' mind raced. *What did I say wrong?*

She spun, eyes gleaming, then dashed away off the quarterdeck.

"Wonderful," Kavros grunted. "She's finally cracked. Well, they say only the mad can sail the Hidden Current to the Halls of the Dead. Maybe we can go there instead."

Manaris grinned. "I've seen that look. That madwoman is about to save your life."

Ven soon sprinted back up onto the deck, her robe hiked up around her ankles with one hand and a battered tome held aloft in the other. "Nautical history! Captain Arbraxis ran aground in this sea in thirteen-seventy-six, which turned out to be a stroke of luck that helped him dodge the Dragon Armada in... Well, never mind that. I know where we are! I can chart a course to Tyr, Erias, even the Halls of the Dead." She stuck out her chin at Kavros.

The three looked to Ulysses, and the weight of their expectation made his shoulders ache.

Ulysses' excitement soured. *But I don't have the wraithleaf. Am I really going to sail into Tyr as a failure?* Ulysses shook those thoughts away. *No. Athareon chose me for a reason. I trusted my crew. I can trust my captain. We'll find a way to help those people.*

"We sail for Tyr. Ven, chart us a course and find out how long we need our rations to last. Kavros, plan accordingly. Manaris, organize the crew. Pair up the doubtful ones with somebody you trust, if you can. Understood?"

Ven's eyes burned bright. "Captain." She nodded before dashing off to her charts.

"Captain." Manaris beamed as he hurried off, calling to men and women as he went.

Kavros turned and grunted, chewing on his lip. "Well, I suppose the Tyrians will be grateful."

Ulysses' face fell. "You know the wraithleaf was destroyed, Kavros."

"*What?*" Kavros roared. "Even the barrels I pulled from the seawater while we dumped the ballast?"

The whole world seemed to come undone and stitch back together in an instant. *Barrels pulled from the seawater? Did that mean...?*

"Why?" Ulysses asked, mouth agape.

Kavros' body tensed. He shrank back and toed the deck with his lame foot. "Orders are orders, sir. Wraithleaf doesn't take well to cold. Some idiots were blabbing about abandoning ship when we ran aground, so I put 'em to good use. I tied 'em down in the crew quarters myself. The medicine, not the idiots." Kavros grimaced as if the words were bile. "And *blight* it, I reckoned if you were the kind of man to care so much about people you'd never met, then who was I to assume you didn't care about the people you had."

"I... I don't know what to say."

"If you don't know what to say, then keep your gob shut!" Kavros barked, face flushed. He paused. "And you're welcome, Captain." He nodded and limped off.

Ulysses watched *Moonlight* come to life again. Rigging went taut and sails shifted, catching the wind and springing to life.

Ven skittered about the deck with her equipment, taking measurements when she could while her baggy robe fluttered about her. Manaris soon ordered the men to move, and a shanty resounded across the deck. Kavros tap-shuffled around the rail of the ship, redirecting men and barking orders.

A predator still, but now *their* predator.

"Sir? What should I do?" Caela asked from behind him.

"What do you want to do?"

She paused for a moment before grinning and sprinting away. Ulysses watched her as she ran towards Manaris.

Something shifted behind her. The fog seemed to change. Ulysses followed the disturbance up from the rail and into the churning darkness. Above, the fog seemed to fight to keep something out as it contorted into shapes and grimacing faces.

It twisted, writhed, and then it failed.

A silver moonbeam cut through the night to alight at Ulysses' feet.

There it is. The light.

A shout rose from the deck. When he looked at the crew, however, they were staring at him, not at the moon. He searched the crowd until he found a grinning Manaris standing with Caela by his side.

Manaris' voice split the air, "All hands, salute!"

Every crew member on deck turned and snapped to attention as one.

Ulysses choked back tears as the salutes devolved into cheering and whooping, and the crew set the sails for Tyr. Ven turned from the salute and began examining her charts once more. Kavros broke his salute slowly and with a curt nod. Manaris wiped away a tear as his hand dropped.

Lastly, Caela smirked from beneath her battered tricorn and mouthed two words.

He caught them, weighed them in his mind as if he might find them to be lies. Then, a rising swell in his chest as they rang true, he whispered them to himself.

"Captain Ulysses."

CALEB RENICH

Caleb Renich grew up on both sides of the ocean, encountering a world that was both harrowing and fantastical through missionary work. Craving stories that do justice to the authentic joy and sorrow of following Christ, Caleb writes theologically rich epic fantasy stories that explore God's nature through magical worlds. Now a proud Nashville resident, he spends his time reading massive epic fantasy doorstoppers (it's for research), wearing flip flops out of season, and trying to find just the right word for "things."

Achievements

- Drafted and edited an 85,000 word novel.

- Operated a writing tutor business for middle and high schoolers.

- Promoted to senior writer and editor-in-chief for a legal marketing firm.

- Launched a Substack account to explore the intersection of fantasy and theology.

- Acquired mentorship at the Realm Makers conference in 2024.

Pitches

- A YA epic fantasy about a boy trying to resurrect his father with ancient magic that once broke the world.

- *Avatar: The Last Airbender* meets Pixar's *Up* in an epic fantasy adventure about a grouchy old man trying to save his city from a colossal space monster.

- An urban fantasy police procedural that is *White Collar* meets *Mistborn: Wax and Wayne*.

"Let me know if you need help inviting people."

Zach swallowed. *People.* "Right."

"I can go with you."

"I'll make the list first." He eased to his feet and headed back down the stone path.

He could feel Alphaeus's serpentine eyes following him.

Zach closed the door behind him and leaned against it with a sigh.

Empty boxes and containers loomed in front of him, and the sink overflowed with cups. How long had things sat this way?

He set the glasses down and gazed at the mess. This had to go.

After an hour or so, he managed to get all the trash into bags and out to his truck.

His back twinged, and he massaged it with a wince. He really needed to rest.

But first, he had to decide who to invite to the party.

He left the dishes in the sink and shuffled to the pile of unopened mail on the coffee table. Dropping onto the couch, he pulled the letters towards him. He flicked junk mail to the side, leaving a small pile of sympathy cards and other letters.

Apparently the Smiths' son had his fifth birthday party last month. And the Nierowskis' daughter had married a sailor.

He'd missed both celebrations.

Frowning, he added their invitations to the pile with some of the sympathy cards. He should probably also invite the neighbors over the hill; they had a bunch of littles who used to visit. Oh, and the Hendersons down the way—they'd brought casseroles when Melody fell ill.

He took a breath and let it out slowly as he reviewed the list of names. There were a lot of people. And he'd have to invite every single one of them.

He sighed. It was already twilight, and he was exhausted. He'd just have to worry about it tomorrow.

After taking a long, hot shower, he clambered into bed and pulled the blankets over him, his hands trembling from the effort. He soon drifted off to sleep.

He awoke feeling like an ogre sat on him. With a groan, he blinked, struggling through the brain fog. He wiped his cheeks and massaged his face.

Why did it have to happen again?

He winced as his back spasmed.

Why did he have to relive that dreadful night in his sleep? Not even loss of consciousness made the awful memory disappear.

With another groan, he pushed upright, arms trembling in protest. He paused, then slid off the bed and to his feet.

Maybe food will help, he thought.

He stumbled to the kitchen, shaking his head to clear it. Jerking open the fridge, he grabbed the first container but quickly tossed it in the trash with a shudder. He sifted through the other leftovers. One after another, he threw them all away.

He closed his eyes and opened them again as his stomach grumbled.

Ice cream and chips sounded great right about now. Just drown the dream in dairy, lay on the couch, and turn on the trashiest show he could find.

She always hated those shows.

He shoved the thought out of his mind, and grabbed the telephone on the stand next to the couch. Pizza was minutes away.

His stomach growled again.

Finally, there was a rap-tap-tap on the door. He opened it.

It wasn't the delivery boy.

"Zacheus?" Alphaeus stood on the porch, looking quizzically up at him.

Zach blinked, then frowned. "What?"

"Weren't you going to town today? It's after ten."

Zach made to close the door. "No."

Alphaeus blocked it. "Zaccheus, you said—"

"I can't go today."

Zach shrugged and finished the dishes. A few mugs would have to wait until tomorrow. He didn't realize he'd used *this* many cups, but they'd be handy for the guests.

After a quick snack, Zach took a hot shower and headed to bed.

"I'll be fine," Zach reassured a watchful Alphaeus. He settled under the covers and closed his eyes, trying to focus on the good memories from the day. Eventually he fell into a fitful sleep.

Halfway through the night, a small, warm form curled up next to him. His face relaxed and his breathing slowed.

Alphaeus laid his head on Zach's chest and fell asleep.

The next morning, Zach awoke to chirping birds, his side oddly warm. He blinked and yawned. He didn't feel brilliantly rested, but at least he couldn't remember the dreams this time. He sat up, rolling his shoulders. Sliding into his gardening overalls, he ate a quick breakfast, and decided it was time to plant the new flowers.

He grabbed his gloves and headed outside.

As the door swung shut behind him, he stumbled and rushed to the railing.

No, no, no. Melody's favorite bush was chewed up and wilted, the plants next to it drooping as bugs swarmed them. He glanced around wildly. Where were they coming from?

He ran to the bush. Squatting down, he saw suspicious white sacks on the leaves. One opened as he watched, and several little bugs wriggled out and began to gnaw on the leaf.

How could he have missed all these? Was he that negligent about his wife's garden?

He stood up and scanned the sky. "Alphaeus!" he shouted.

A moment later Alphaeus dropped from the sky to his shoulder. "What is it?"

"Melody's bush!"

Alphaeus stared. "When did this start?"

"I don't know! They're going to eat the whole garden. I'll have to cancel the party."

"I'll see if any of the neighbors can help us. We can still save this. The party will be fine. Just stay here and see if you can keep the pests away from the other bushes." Alphaeus took off.

Zach watched him leave, praying he'd be successful. It was all falling apart around him.

He yelped as he noticed another plant sagging beneath the oncoming horde. Hobbling over to the hose, he squeaked the valve open, unwound layer upon layer of the great snake and dragged it to the bush. He unleashed the torrent to drive the bugs back. Except he could only spray so many places at once. They seemed to spread faster than he could turn.

He growled in frustration and squeezed the trigger harder.

The minutes crawled by.

Finally, Alphaeus returned.

"The neighbor over the hill has the same plant, and they're home," Alphaeus called as he lit upon one of the bush's bare branches. "They're willing to help us and are familiar with the bush." He nabbed a passing bug and gulped it down.

"Thank you," Zach huffed. "Let's go." He dropped the hose and met Alphaeus at the truck.

Alphaeus directed him down the road and past the trees to a red-shingled house with vibrant flowers and bushes blanketing the surrounding meadow. Zach turned into the driveway and parked. He knocked on the front door and prayed the owner could help him.

A kindly woman with a flour-sprinkled apron opened the door. Her brow wrinkled for a moment, but then her face dimpled as she smiled.

"Oh! You must be the fellow this lovely dragon was talking about, with the azalea?" She peered closer. "Pardon me, but you look familiar. Where did you say you live?"

Alphaeus nudged his foot.

"Just down the road," Zach coughed. "I'm Zach. My azalea's infested with pests, and they're spreading to the rest of the garden. Can you help?"

"Oh! Absolutely." She paused and frowned. "Zach, you said?" Her eyes widened. "Zacheus Ebenezer? Melody's husband?"

Zach froze. "Yes...?"

"I'm Rosa! We loved Melody. We were so sad when she passed. The kids had such fun in her garden. I'm sorry it's struggling today. Let me see how we can help." She brushed off her hands. "Follow me." She led him behind the house, asking him about the pests.

He didn't know how to answer.

Rosa paused in front of the shed and pulled the door open. She then turned back to the house and called, "Ginger! Thomas! Adeline! Come help me, please." She returned to the shed and pulled things off the shelves. A second later three children appeared, glancing curiously at Zach as they passed him.

They emerged from the shed carrying an assortment of bags, sprays, and small buckets.

Zach started forward. "Do you need help?"

Rosa hesitated on the step. "Thomas, how would you feel about going ahead with Mr. Ebenezer?"

Zach's eyes widened. He'd never had a kid in his truck before.

"In the truck in the driveway?" the freckled boy asked, eyes brightening.

"Sure."

"Okay. Mr. Ebenezer, if you can take these sprays, we'll be in business."

He accepted the bottles and led the way to the truck, dazed. "What—what do I owe you?"

"For the Ebenezers, we'd do anything. No protests allowed," she said firmly.

"Thank you," Zach said.

They loaded his truck with the buckets and spray bottles, then the boy hopped in while the girls loaded the minivan parked in the garage.

"Okay. Thomas will show you what to do with the spray and buckets. If you're comfortable, Mr. Ebenezer, could we share some of our plants with you?

They're effective preventatives when paired with the azalea, and we have extra sprouts."

"If you're sure—yes, thank you," Zach said.

"Okay! Go ahead with Thomas, and we'll be right behind you." She waved them off.

A few minutes later a silent Zach and an excited Thomas were back at the cottage. Thomas helped him unload, then filled the small buckets with soapy water from the kitchen sink. He handed Zach a spray bottle and took a bucket over to the azalea, where he began knocking bugs into the mixture.

They'd made good progress by the time Rosa arrived with her two daughters.

Zach stared at the treasure trove they unloaded from her minivan: orange and yellow flowers, herbs, and mint, among other things. Including a picnic basket. "This is too much," he said, chest aching. "How much do I *really* owe you?"

"Don't even think about it! You two gave so much to this community and to my family. Please let us give back."

Zach's throat constricted. He nodded and helped unload.

Then they got to work, taking a break halfway through for the lunch Rosa had packed.

Zach bit into his sandwich and immediately questioned his earlier desire to stay inside. What had she put in it? It was better than anything he'd eaten in years. Maybe Alphaeus had a point about socializing.

They resumed the battle against the bugs until finally, only stragglers remained. The new plants were settled in the ground, and as the sun set, Zach stood over the last of them with the hose, exhausted and covered in dirt.

"Thank you," Zach said as Rosa and her kids packed up. Alphaeus nudged him again. "Hey." Rosa glanced back. "I'm—I'm throwing a garden party tomorrow for Melody's birthday. It was something she wanted to do. Would you come?"

"We'd love to! We were just going to hang out with the Joneses tomorrow, but if it's all right with you we can bring them with us here instead. It would mean a lot to celebrate Melody."

Zach dipped his head. "Please. I meant to send invitations, but…"

"It's okay! If any of them are close by, we can drop some off on our way back."

"If it's not too much," Zach said. "I don't have them all ready yet, but I can get you the list, if that's all right."

"Of course!"

Zach hobbled inside and gathered all the names on a notepad. He brought it to Rosa, who looked it over and copied the names she knew who were nearby. It was a good number from the list.

"I really appreciate this," Zach said.

"It's no trouble. Most of them aren't too far out of our way, and it'd be great to visit with them again!"

Then they were off. Zach wearily climbed the porch steps and headed inside. He opened a window so Alphaeus could come and go as he pleased, and skipped dinner in favor of a shower.

By the time he crawled into bed, he was too tired to even dream.

The next morning dawned bright and cheerful, the sunlight stabbing his eyes until he got up. He groggily gathered breakfast.

Alphaeus greeted him before heading out.

"Do you think you could invite some other neighbors while you're out hunting this morning?" Zach asked.

Alphaeus glanced at him. "Anyone in particular?"

"Maybe the last few people on the list. But I trust you."

Alphaeus nodded, scaly brow raised. "That was good work yesterday," he added softly. "You did well with the family."

"Thanks." Zach watched him leave, then washed the dishes and shuffled out to the porch. He took a deep breath and let the sun and fresh scents wash over him. He looked out onto a brightly vivid garden and blinked.

Shimmering threads wove between flowers and bushes, blooms brightening as the magic danced past. And there—the tell-tale chimes of the fairies returning to the garden. He grinned.

The magic was back.

And he could see it.

The azalea still looked battle-worn, but it had perked up overnight, and the new plants had settled well. He nodded, pleased to see the garden healing. It was incredible the amount of difference a few flowers—and friends—could make.

He returned to the kitchen to make the raspberry-lemon cake, humming.

Memories bubbled up inside him.

Her favorite cake. For her first birthday that he'd celebrate without her.

But she'd be so proud of him. And he knew she'd like what they'd done with the garden. It looked lovely and the neighbors would get to enjoy it.

Eventually everything was ready. He'd put out the cake and snacks, Melody's mug collection, and the lemonade. Her little table sat on the porch next to her worn rocking chair, a cup of lemonade and a dainty plate by a little framed portrait of her lovely, smiling face. He sat next to her, tracing her picture, and waited.

He didn't wait long. Gravel crunched as Rosa and her kids arrived with the Joneses. Then came several families Zach hadn't seen in years, some of them bringing extra snacks and blankets to share. He watched, heart full, as the garden came alive with cheery voices and laughing children.

Everyone stopped to pay respects at Melody's chair.

Zach nodded as Alphaeus perched on its back.

Then it was time to cut the cake. He gave Melody the first slice and raised his glass. "To Melody."

Everyone toasted her with their lemonade, and the kids drained theirs in seconds and clamored for more. Zach obliged them, filling the proffered cups, which promptly vanished.

Then Zach gave Alphaeus his own slice, with extra raspberries on top. After Alphaeus finished his cake and lemonade, he zipped around the garden, letting the kids chase him. Then he returned and settled on Melody's table in obvious exhaustion.

Zach raised his glass to the empty chair. "For you, my love," he said quietly.

Alphaeus stirred and curled more tightly around her cup, his tail underlining the words engraved on the picture frame: *In Melody's Memory.*

SURFACE PROTOCOL: AVOID ALL WATER

KARA HATT

IV drip.

He leaned his forehead on the glass and sighed.

A green hand appeared in the corner of his eye. It was Jasper.

"I do want to help her," Ferdinand said. "I do."

"I believe you, and little Ame told me about what happened. Look, here's the important thing to remember. It's the dry season. The chances of us encountering water are slim. And once we arrive at the river valley, I'll get the Syrithol, not you. To remove wild Syrithol I will dig two inches wide around the base, cut the stem at three inches and leave five inches of root. Once transplanted, I will cultivate it till the shipment arrives. You can just watch as far away as you want."

Ferdinand sighed. *Is this it? These are my options?*

Objectively, it all sounded like a safe plan knowing the valley's geography. Yet, the thought of getting anywhere near the river was still nauseating. *He said I could stand as far away as I wanted to. I can live with that.*

He looked back at Ame. "Okay, I'll do it. As long as I don't go near the river."

"Very, well. Oh, and your parents have asked me to drive the quad."

For the first time that morning, Ferdinand grinned.

12:15pm

Ferdinand held his breath as the hanger doors lifted, and the platform extended out. Dust blew as it settled on the ground. His eyes ached as they adjusted to the sun's rays. Not a puddle of water in sight. The quad lurched forward, and he clung to Jasper's back on their bumpy trip down the side of the mesa.

Since this part of the planet was often subject to frequent, dangerous flooding, the medical ship was docked on top of a mesa. Off-road vehicles were the fastest means of transport to and from the plateau.

Ferdinand missed the fun of fast off-road driving. He used to do it when he volunteered to help his parents provide medical care in Ame's hometown, before it was wrecked by a local flood a few months ago.

After speeding down the cliff side for an hour, the remains of the town came into view.

Hey, it looks like the clean-up efforts are working.

The floodwater had been drained from the strip malls and town square. The suburban area, however, was a wreckage to behold. Even the metal streetlamps and signs were gone.

The workers had created narrow pathways on the roads, but all the debris was stacked in large piles of twisted metal and water-soaked wood. How was he going to find Ame's house? It was near the garden park where the path to the valley began, but even that was gone or buried.

He closed his eyes to form a mental picture. The entrance to the suburbs was marked by a bridge that went over the main street for pedestrians as opposed to using the crosswalks.

"Let's find the bridge first," he suggested to Jasper.

They did, and somehow it was still standing. *Thank goodness!* And they hadn't encountered water at all. *So far so good.*

Together they counted three streets down from the bridge, then a left, then a right. There on the corner sat the ruins of Ame's house. He pictured what the inside of it used to look like. The sleepovers and pillow fights. The couch forts they used to build and houses to play imaginary games like "town." Ame often pretended to be the mayor, and he was the sheriff or a firefighter. Her parents' vegetable garden was the "wild wood" where the game often veered into fantasy where they fought mythical creatures from Elysian legends.

A tinge of sadness started to build in his chest as the weight of reality set in.

Ame's family lost everything in the disaster and now her life was on the line.

"So," Jasper said, interrupting his thoughts, "where is the garden park?"

"If we go down this street for a little bit we should see an archway. That's the entrance." *Please, let it still be there,* Ferdinand prayed.

Jasper drove a little bit longer and Ferdinand began to wonder if they missed the entrance. Maybe the arch had been destroyed. It was made out of wood, do flips on. It used to be their fun spot to swim until the sudden flash flood swooshed over him.

He remembered the darkness. The pain in his lungs as he tried not to breathe. He vaguely remembered Ame grabbing both his arms and pulling him up. Jumping back into the river was dangerous, yet she had been brave and saved his life.

She was brave for me then; I can be brave for her now.

He clenched his fists. Still shaking, but somehow he willed his limbs to be calm. He nodded at Jasper.

"All right, let's roll."

Jasper tied the rope around him and guided him to the strongest branch.

"Okay, here's the plan. You're gonna crawl across to the other side first. Then I'll throw you my bag. It has all my gardening tools in it, a burlap sack, and plastic containers for you to pick as many berries as you can. Do you know how to transplant a herb?"

"I do. I help in the spaceship's greenery all the time."

"Good. Once you're done with that, put everything into the bag. It'll be heavy, so you won't be able to carry it back on your own. Tie the rope around it so I can pull it back to me, then you're next. Understood?"

"Yes, sir."

Jasper patted him on the back.

Ferdinand looked down at the blue dragon's trunk which lay at a downward angle to the island. It'd been dead for a while. All that remained were dead, bleached out branches.

He descended feet first, half-shimmying, half crawling down the trunk. He dared not to look at the river beneath. Instead, he kept his eyes on Jasper to make sure his lifeline was still secure. The rope tugged on his waist. Just like rock climbing.

"Look down at your feet, child." Jasper commanded.

He did. And a wave of fear rushed over him upon seeing the rapids. He desperately tried to keep his eyes on his muddy boots and any dead branches to use as footholds.

He took deep breaths. *You're okay. You're okay. You're still on the tree.*

Before descending past the tree's thickest limbs Ferdinand turned over on his belly and scooted down the main trunk until his back hit the tree's roots.

Jasper whistled, and the backpack soared through the air.

Ferdinand caught it just before it slammed into his face.

Time to go to work.

He jumped down from the trunk. Grabbing a plastic container, he picked as many berries as he could. These would be used for the patients who needed the Purithorn syrup immediately. The berries also contained seeds, but a plant would be the quickest way to reproduce more.

"Ferdinand!"

He looked up.

"Stop picking the berries. You have to get the herb now!"

He looked down at the bank. The water had risen quicker than he expected. It lapped near the tree's base. With haste he got out Jasper's trowel, trimmers, a burlap sack, and a small measuring tape. *To remove wild Syrithol dig two inches wide around the base, cut the stem at three inches and leave five inches of root.*

He tried to meticulously measure it, but he didn't have time. It was a risk, but he had to eyeball it. *I hope I don't accidentally kill this plant!* He placed it carefully into the burlap sack, put everything back in the bag, and rushed towards the tree. His boots began to sink in the mud. He quickly scaled the roots.

Jasper was right. The backpack was heavy.

"Hurry. Tie the rope."

He grabbed the end of his lifeline as he realized… It was either him or the backpack. Scaling the tree without it would be dangerous if he fell. *Ame was brave, too.* He did as Jasper said. Jasper pulled the backpack back to shore.

"Alright, Ferdinand. You're next."

Water droplets splattered on his shins. The hair raised on his arms. The rapids were right at his feet. *I need to climb, now!* He scaled the trunk like a speedy lizard.

"Come on, child! Come on!" Jasper yelled. "Grab my hand!"

Ferdinand reached out, and Jasper yanked onto the other side. He flopped on the dry ground and watched the thin clouds crawl across the sky. Jasper unzipped the backpack. He lifted his head, his face shining with glee.

"You did it, my child! You did it!"

Ferdinand's head fell back. Then reality hit. *I just did it! I got the Syrithol. Ame's might be cured in time!*

The pair hastened their way back to the medical ship.

Ferdinand sat beside Ame's bed inside Quarantine.

He relayed to her what happened three days ago over a game of checkers.

"I saw our rock, by the way. And you know, I think I might want to go back. Or even your neighborhood's lake."

"It's been forever since you said that."

Ferdinand put a finger in the air. "But after we ride on the quad."

Ame laughed. He'd never take for granted the sweetness of seeing his friend laugh or even smile. It made her grey eyes turn silver. He didn't know the exact biology of it, but it was good to see them shimmer like that after being swollen shut for two days. Her sores also receded into tiny red dots. Some would scar, but even they would heal over after a good sauna treatment to restore her skin's water membrane.

"I knew that was coming."

Someone tapped on the window. Ame threw the covers off her bed.

"Mother. Father. Uncle," she said.

Ame put her hand on the window, and her family did the same.

Ferdinand leaned back in his chair. After gazing upon their once-again vibrant daughter, her mother and father looked at Ferdinand who sat himself up a little taller. He couldn't hear them through the glass, but they clearly said, "Thank you."

He smiled and nodded back at them.

No words could describe how proud he was to have taken the chance to save his best friend.

KARA HATT

Ever since Kara Hatt entered the realm of Narnia and encountered Aslan, she's created many fantastical worlds where encountering truth can be a radical experience. Since then she's wanted to tell stories that give space for Christians to ponder burning questions while affirming the values of their faith. She found Ted Dekker's novels in high school and was further inspired by his writing skill and thematic storytelling. When Kara is not working on her novel she can be found riding her mountain bike, brainstorming a new short story, or brushing up on a new theology book.

Achievements

- Completed three full-length novels, a novella, and multiple short stories

- Completed Ted Dekker's creative writing course, The Creative Way.

- Implemented developmental edits from professional editors.

- Extensive training in platform-building and creating an author newsletter.

- Launched two business ventures to practice marketing skills, including an email marketing consulting business.

- Graduated from two-years of ministry school and received The Eagle Award from her private Christian high school for greatest demonstration of Christlikeness, servanthood, and being led by the Spirit.

Pitches

- *Indiana Jones: Raiders of the Lost Ark* meets *Tuck Everlasting* in a Christian YA action/adventure where a 19-year-old girl must find the Living Blueprint - a fountain of youth legend - to cure her terminally-ill grandma who only has one month to live.

Historical
Young Adult

SUMMER STONES
MEGAN WALTERS

Bayside, Michigan
June 1953

Stones covered the top of Otto's dresser in a precise pattern, sorted by mineral composition. Surveying himself in the mirror above the dresser, he adjusted the collar of his blue and green checked shirt then took a comb to his damp, spiky hair.

"Looking more alive there, pal," Otto told his reflection. "Good thing, 'cause we've got a lotta work to do." He made a face at the faint spots yet to fade from his cheeks. A week and half lost because he'd gotten sick—with chickenpox of all things! Nobody who's seventeen ought to be getting chickenpox. Shaking his head, he consulted the lighthouse calendar next to the mirror.

Tomorrow morning was his last chance to enter his project for the science fair. He glanced over at the half-finished display on his desk. Today, he needed to edit his notes on agate formation, draw up the finalized diagrams, and find a piece of agate to display with it all.

The geology professor from Oak Ridge, Dr. Winkler, was going to be one of the judges, and Otto hoped he'd do well enough to catch Dr. Winkler's attention, which would, hopefully, give him a leg up in the world of geology.

A knock sounded on his door. "Otto?"

"Come in, Mom," he called, setting his comb down and hunting for a pair of socks in the top drawer of the dresser.

The door swung open with a soft squeak.

"Are you feeling better this morning?" His mother touched his cheek with the back of her hand and gave him a once over.

"Fit as a fiddle. How do I look?"

"Like you're about to leave the house with mismatched socks."

Looking at the socks in his hand, he tossed them back into the drawer with a sigh and pulled out a matching pair. "Are these better?"

"Yes, dear. Breakfast will be ready soon." With an amused smile, she left the room. After pulling on his socks, Otto went out and set the breakfast table, then settled in the living room with a *Popular Science* magazine.

"Otto, *what* are you wearing? It's so... *average.*"

Otto glanced up. Ever since Hazel turned fifteen, she had decided she was responsible for the appearance of the entire family. "Well, I happen to be rather average, dear sister."

"It's time for breakfast," Hazel said, rolling her eyes. Her hibiscus patterned skirt flounced as she went to the dining room. Setting aside his magazine, Otto passed his dad talking on the telephone and went to the table, sitting across from Stella, his little sister, who still wore a striped nightgown.

"Morning, Otto!" she said as she snuck a piece of bacon to the sassy bug-eyed calico cat under the table.

"Hey, Stella." Otto grabbed some toast from the plate his mother passed to him as his father walked into the room.

"Well, Jake called in 'sick' again. Honestly, I should fire him. Pass the orange juice, would you, dear? Otto, do you have anything going on today? I could use a hand sweeping the shop." Dad pointed at him with a piece of bacon, eyebrows raised.

"Aw, Dad, sorry, I need to finish up my science fair project." As much as Otto hated sweeping up hair clippings at the barber shop, it was pretty rotten luck to have Jake skip out, and Dad was the last person he wanted to disappoint. "I was hoping to go to the beach to look for a piece of agate to display with my project."

"Oh, that's right. Never mind then."

"Can I go, Otto?" Stella asked, her glass of orange juice sloshing as she thumped it down on the table.

"Not this time, squirt. Maybe later." Ruffling her hair, Otto shoveled in the last of his scrambled eggs, grabbed his dishes, and took them to the kitchen.

Making two peanut butter sandwiches, he stuffed them in a paper bag, then filled his dad's old army canteen with tap water.

In his room, he grabbed a decommissioned paper route bag and tossed in his lunch, his wallet, a notebook, and a few pencils. Slipping on his brown and white saddle shoes, he headed back out to the living room.

"I'm going to the beach, Mom," he hollered from the front door.

"Be back in time for dinner!"

Sunshine splashed the front of the house and a cool breeze tugged the storm door shut behind Otto as he crossed the porch with a cheery whistle. Tilting his pine and lime Western Super Flyer bicycle away from the house, he checked the tires.

The front was nice and firm, but the bottom of the back tire sagged onto the grass like molten rock. Dropping his bag on the ground with a sigh, Otto went to the garage and dug out a tire pump. He carried it to his bike and twisted off the cap on the tire.

"Hi, Otto! Are you feeling better?"

He looked up. His neighbor, Lizzie, stood on the sidewalk with her butter-yellow Schwinn. She wore a bright red bandana patterned shirt tucked into a pair of rolled up denim slacks. Cherry-colored Keds matched the little bows at the end of her braids.

"Hey, Lizzie. Yeah, I'm feeling better. Thanks for asking." He fitted the end of the hose to the tire and started pumping.

"Flat tire, huh?" Lizzie shook her head. "That's too bad. Do you need help?"

"Nah, I got it." Otto paused and tested the tire. It was firmer, but an audible hiss came from the bottom of the tire, and it started to deflate again. "Rats."

"Maybe you could patch it?"

"I used the last patch on Stella's bike a few weeks ago, and the spare's busted, too." Resting his elbow on his knee, Otto rubbed his chin. "Now what?"

"You can borrow Jim's bike, if you want," Lizzie said. "I don't think he'll mind."

"Um, I don't know…"

"Aw, come on. He's on a navy cruiser in the middle of the ocean. He's not using it."

Otto shook his head. "Nah, I'll just walk."

"Where are you going?" she asked.

"To the beach."

"Really? I'm heading there myself." She gestured to the basket on the front of her bike. Inside lay a folded sheet, a crocheted bag, a thermos, and a portable Westinghouse radio. "You can ride my bike, and I'll sit on the handlebars."

"That's okay, Lizzie, I'll just walk. But thanks for offering." Otto adjusted his bag and set off down the sidewalk. In one smooth motion, Lizzie hopped on her bike and pushed off, whizzing past him.

Circling back, she coasted along beside him. "Are you going swimming?"

"No, I'm going to look for a piece of agate for my project for the science fair."

"Oh, I can't wait to see your project, Otto. I'm sure it'll be great." Lizzie grinned and picked up her pace. "I'll keep an eye out for any agates while I'm combing the beach. See you later!"

By the time Otto reached the beach, Lizzie had laid out a flowered sheet on the sand, the things from her bike basket anchoring the corners against the breeze. The radio played *Love Letters in the Sand*, a song Otto considered rather cheesy.

Taking his bag over to a picnic table, Otto pulled off his shoes and socks and rolled up his pant legs. Burying his feet in the still-cool sand, he surveyed the beach.

Lake Michigan shimmered in the sun, and the radio's tune wove its way across the sparkling sand. Lizzie wandered along the shoreline toward the pier, a shiny silver bucket glinting in her hand. So far the beach was empty. It was still too early in the day for tourists.

Gulls cried out above Otto as he headed down the beach to the fence that separated the public space from private property. At the water's edge, smooth sand gave way to rocks. Using a stick, Otto sectioned off a small square and started methodically searching for agate, waves lapping at the stones.

Red and white quartz, bluish-gray chert, green and pink unakite. He worked his way across the lakefront, and found a few tiny pieces of agate, but nothing like what he'd hoped for.

"Find anything yet?" Lizzie's voice traveled down the beach as she ran toward him, her bucket clinking as it banged against her leg.

Drawing another square, Otto shook his head. "No, not yet."

She slowed down, looking at his sections. "You're very... exact about it."

"Mm-hm." Fractured brown and white lightning stones, black fossil soup, porous yellow sandstone.

"I found these. Will they help?" Kneeling beside him, she held out a few stones: two orange agates smaller than her fingernail and a curved piece of pale blue chalcedony.

"I was looking for something bigger. Something that will stand out and really grab the judges' attention." Otto pointed at the chalcedony. "And that isn't agate."

"Well, no, but it was pretty and kind of close." She shrugged and dropped the stones in her pail. "I'll go look some more."

Otto watched Lizzie's braids bounce against her shoulders as she skipped away.

The sun had risen higher, and more people had arrived.

A few teenagers started a game of volleyball while a rather pale bald man with a newspaper sat in a low chair, dozing in the sunshine, seemingly unaware that several small children were burying him in sand. Lizzie stopped to talk to a group of girls building a sandcastle and rummaged around in her bucket. She gave them some rocks to decorate it with before continuing her search for more treasures along the shore.

Otto turned back to his own search and drew another square.

Otto's hands and knees hurt from kneeling on the sand. Silica crystals and tiny pebbles pressed into his palms, leaving imprints. His pants were wet and sandy from the constant ebb and flow of the lake's waves, and while he'd found some little bits of agate here and there, none if it was what he was looking for.

With an annoyed sigh, he sat cross-legged and took a swig from his canteen, glancing at his watch. *Almost noon.* He stood and went over to the table and pulled out his lunch then took a bite of a peanut butter sandwich, chasing it down with another gulp from the canteen.

Lizzie came over and plopped next to him on the bench. "How's it going?"

Otto shrugged. "Not great. I haven't found anything."

"Would this work?" She pulled a pinkish-red agate from her bucket.

"It's a little too small," he said.

She wrinkled her nose and squinted at him. "What do you mean it's too small? It's as big as nickel. It's probably the biggest one on the beach!"

"I'd just rather have something bigger." He stuffed another bite in his mouth.

Lizzie rolled her eyes and pulled out another stone, dark red and shiny as a beetle wing. "What about this?"

"That's jasper," he said.

"Well, yes, but isn't it kind of like agate? It's bigger at least."

"I can't really use jasper for my project about agate formation." Otto wadded up his lunch bag. "It's okay, I'll just keep looking by myself. It'll be easier that way."

Lizzie cocked her head at him. "Why do you think you have to do it all by yourself?"

Otto sighed. "When Mike and I worked together for that project last year, he didn't do what he said he would. I had to do extra work to make up for our bad grade." He kicked at the sand. "Besides, that's what scientists do. Have you ever seen a paper or a project with two names on it?"

Lizzie shrugged. "I don't know."

"The answer is 'no.' Scientists work alone, and if I'm going to be a scientist, I have to rely on myself."

She raised a skeptical eyebrow. "I'm not so sure about that, Otto. My Uncle Elmer has assisted a few of the professors at Oak Ridge before, and they're scientists."

Otto's eyes widened. "Your Uncle Elmer? As in Mr. Elmer Jackson, who puts up those geology displays at the library every month?"

Lizzie nodded.

"Do you think he might have an agate I could borrow?"

"Maybe," she said with a smile. "Let's go ask!"

Mr. Jackson's house was an old Victorian with new coats of pink and blue paint.

Otto and Lizzie approached, and Lizzie leaned her bike against the big white porch.

Skipping up the steps, she pulled the door open and stuck her head inside. "Hello? Uncle Elmer? It's Lizzie, and I brought a friend."

A muffled response came from somewhere inside the house.

"Come on," she said, beckoning for Otto to follow. When he hesitated, she grabbed his hand and pulled him in. "Aw, don't be shy. Uncle Elmer loves visitors."

Otto just nodded and went after her, farther into the house— coming face to face with a mounted boar head.

"What—?" He stumbled back.

"Oh, that's Algernon. Don't worry. He doesn't bite." Lizzie winked and tugged him away. They went down a hall to a workroom where Mr. Jackson hovered over a table.

Shelves displaying rocks and minerals lined the walls.

"Hello, Uncle Elmer!"

Mr. Jackson looked up from the dissected gizmo spread out in front of him. "How's my favorite niece?"

"Just peachy! This is my friend Otto. Wait—" Lizzie quirked an eyebrow at Otto. "Are we friends?"

"Um, I s-suppose..."

"Well, we're neighbors at any rate. Otto, this is my uncle, Mr. Jackson."

Adjusting his horn-rimmed glasses, Mr. Jackson shook Otto's hand heartily. "Nice to meet you, Supposed Friend Otto."

Otto smiled. "Nice to meet you, sir. I've really admired your displays at the library."

"Thank you. I enjoy them as well."

"Otto is a geologist," Lizzie announced.

"Is that so?"

"Well, I enjoy geology," Otto clarified.

"Then, you're halfway there," Mr. Jackson said.

"He's entering the science fair tomorrow, and he needs a piece of agate to display with it." Lizzie twirled on a stool at her uncle's workbench. "Do you have one he could borrow?"

Mr. Jackson rubbed his chin. "Really? What's your project about, Otto?"

"It's about the formation of agate." With a grin, Otto pulled his notebook from his bag and flipped it open. "Agate is a microcrystalline form of quartz, characterized by its banded appearance and wide range of colors." He explained that the bands were created by silica rich fluid and how the presence of different minerals created different colors.

"Very nice. I can tell you've done your research," Mr. Jackson said as he looked over the diagram sketches in his notebook.

"I hope to study under Dr. Winkler after high school, and since he's going to be one of the judges, I really want to catch his attention."

"Of course! Dr. Winkler is a fine geologist. We've worked together in the past." Setting down Otto's notebook, Mr. Jackson turned to a curio cabinet in the corner of the room. "Now, then, let me see... Ah, here we are." He pulled out a small white box and set it on the workbench in front of Otto. "Go ahead. Open it."

Otto worked off the lid. Inside was a sunset-colored agate the size of a robin's egg nestled against white cotton. "Holy mackerel! Where did you find this?"

"Over along Lake Superior a few years back. It was covered in muck, and I almost passed it over. Good thing I didn't."

"And I can really borrow it?"

"Sure. Just give it back when you're done." Mr. Jackson winked at him.

"Otto," Lizzie said slowly, looking over his notebook, "this is your project?"

"Yes, why?"

"Well..." She bit her lip. "Milton was bragging about how great his project was going to be, and yours sounds a lot like it."

"What?" Otto deflated like his bicycle tire. "Are you sure?"

"Yes. It's all he talked about last week."

Otto groaned and slumped into a chair. Of course it would be Milton Hayes, that know-it-all teacher's pet.

Mr. Jackson patted him on the shoulder. "Don't worry about it too much. I'm sure you'll think of a way to stand out." Waving Lizzie over to a table in the middle of the room, he asked her to show him what she found at the beach.

As Lizzie pulled the small pail from her bag, Otto picked up the little white box and looked at the agate. This was just terrible. It would seem like he copied off Milton, which was the last thing he wanted to do.

"Hmph. All that work for nothing," he muttered, setting the agate down. Dr. Winkler would not be impressed if his project was the same as Milton's. *Now what?* He meandered over to where Lizzie was showing her uncle her collection.

"... and I found this Petoskey stone." She held up a small gray pebble. Licking her thumb, she rubbed the rock, revealing a hexagon pattern on the surface. "See? Petoskey stones are fossilized coral."

Mr. Jackson peered through a pair of spectacles. "Very nice, Lizzie. Let's see... tell me about these ones." He pointed to two stones and a piece of frosty blue glass.

"This is just a piece of glass that was tossed around in the lake for a long time until the edges were worn down. But these two unakites get their pink and green coloring from feldspar and epidote."

"I didn't realize you were interested in geology, Lizzie," Otto said.

Lizzie shrugged. "Not really. I just like the rocks because they're pretty, and Uncle Elmer thought I should learn about them."

Otto took a closer look at her findings. Most of them were small and had flaws, but they *were* pretty.

"I'm sorry Milton had the same idea as you. Is there anything I can do to help?" Lizzie asked.

"I dunno. I'm not really sure what to do now." Otto pointed to some of her stones. "Can you tell me about these ones?"

Eyes sparkling like sun-laced sand, Lizzie gave him a rundown of her rocks. She knew a lot, and her voice held so much excitement, as if the most common stones had value just because they were beautiful.

It inspired him.

As she finished with a piece of gneiss, Otto said, "What if, instead of one rock, I make my project about a lot of them." He gestured to her treasures on the table. "It could be a showcase of some of the different rocks in Lake Michigan and their compositions. Would you like to help me?"

"Sure!" Sweeping her stones aside, Lizzie grabbed a pen from the workbench and Otto's notebook. "Let's make a list of the things you can find in Lake Michigan. Uncle Elmer?" She looked around. "I wonder where he went. We can ask him for some research material."

"How about these?" Mr. Jackson entered the room, his arms full of books.

Otto eyed the volumes. "I guess I'd better get reading."

"Is twelve too many?" Otto asked, looking over their narrowed-down list.

"I don't think so." Lizzie held up a piece of cardboard she'd found and folded the sides into the middle. "We could do three on each side and six in the center."

"I like it. I'll work on writing up the notes. Do you want to... work on a layout for the display?" He'd seen Lizzie's art projects from school and knew she had an eye for design.

"I'd love to!" She rummaged around in her uncle's workbench for supplies while Otto started jotting down what he knew about each of the rocks they'd chosen.

Lightning stones, also known as septarian nodules, are shades of brown with white "lightning..."

"There, all finished." Lizzie smoothed away a drip of glue with her finger.

Otto had made cards out of pasteboard for the facts about each rock, and she had put a red and blue border around each of them.

Otto grinned. "It looks great."

Mr. Jackson looked up from a book. "Very nice, Otto and Lizzie."

Otto and Lizzie. Otto glanced at the top of the display board. Under the title *Rocks of Lake Michigan and Their Composition*, Lizzie had written *By Otto Edwards*. But she contributed just as much work as he did. She had added beauty to his facts and information, making his project better than what he could've done on his own.

"Lizzie, we should add your name to the top, too." He grabbed one of the pens and handed it to her. "By Otto Edwards and Lizzie Brown."

She shook her head. "That's okay, Otto. I don't need my name on it. You did all the hard work."

He frowned. "Are you sure?"

"Yes. I'm happy to help, and I don't need credit." She gave him the pen back.

"I think you will find," Mr. Jackson said, "that there are a lot of people behind the scenes who prefer to keep it that way. Scientists often have assistants who stay out of the limelight until they can make a name for themselves."

"Really?" Otto never considered that. But then, he thought back to the magazine he had read that morning. Some of the articles did mention scientists *and* their assistants. Plus, many people had edited, formatted, printed, and distributed the magazine. Without all of them, no one would learn about the latest discoveries.

Mr. Jackson glanced at his watch. "You kids better get on home before your mothers start calling. The last thing I need is Suzie Brown and Vera Edwards givin' me an earful."

Incandescent streetlights flickered to life, and fireflies winked as the sun faded from the sky. Otto pedaled Lizzie's bike while she rode on the handlebars.

"Well, here we are," Otto said as they stopped outside Lizzie's house. The windows glowed, and a yard light illuminated the driveway.

Lizzie hopped off the handlebars and pulled her things out of the basket, setting them on the porch. "Can you help me with the garage door?"

"Sure." Wheeling the bike down the driveway, Otto helped her raise the door, and Lizzie parked her bike next to the blue convertible inside.

"Do you want to take Jim's bike for tomorrow?" she asked.

Otto hesitated, then nodded. "Sure, if he won't mind."

"Nope. And even if he did, he'd never know unless you scratched it." She grabbed the handlebars of a shiny red and white Firestone Super Cruiser and brought it out as Otto closed the door.

"You're going to bring those specimens, right?"

"Fossil soup, puddingstone, Petoskey, and rhyolite." Lizzie counted them on her fingers. "Was that all of them?"

"Yes, and thanks for your help. I'd look like a copycat if it weren't for you." He stuck his hand out.

Laughing, she rolled her eyes and shook it. "You're welcome. Thanks for letting me tag along." She took a breath, sobering for a moment, then smiled softly. "I've been kind of lonely since Jim left so it was nice to do something with somebody." Otto grabbed the handlebars of Jim's bike, and they walked up the driveway together.

From the sidewalk, Otto watched her climb the porch steps. "I'm glad you came, Lizzie," he called.

She waved as she gathered her things and went inside.

The next morning, Otto carefully put the stones he needed in a small box and covered them with cotton batting. Slipping the box in the saddle bag of Jim's bike, he hopped on and rode over to Lizzie's house.

Mr. Brown was in the driveway giving his already shiny convertible an extra coat of polish. "Morning, Otto," he called.

"Good morning, Mr. Brown. Is Lizzie up?"

Before Mr. Brown could respond, Lizzie came flying out of the house carrying a pair of white shoes. Her bright red Keds clashed with her mint green dress. "I just need to grab my bike," she called as she raced to the garage and put her shoes in her bike's basket. "Bye, Daddy. See you later!"

Otto followed Lizzie as she shot down the sidewalk on her bike. When they reached Bayside High School, Mr. Jackson was already there. "You better hurry. They just called thirty more minutes to set up."

Otto parked his bike next to Lizzie's while she changed her shoes and slipped on a pair of white gloves.

"Let's go," she said, grabbing her purse. Otto fished his box from the saddle bag and followed them into the gymnasium where tables and projects filled the room.

"Here's your spot," Mr. Jackson said, pointing to a table where their display

lay on its back. Otto stood it up and took out the stones, placing them in their compartments while Lizzie filled the empty spots with her rocks.

"Doesn't it look nice?" Lizzie asked.

Otto took a step back and surveyed his project. "I think it looks great," he said with a grin.

"Good luck, Otto," Mr. Jackson said, giving him a slap on the back. "I'm off to look around."

Otto offered his arm to Lizzie. "Shall we take a gander at the competition?"

Slipping the handle of her purse over her wrist, she took his arm. "I'd love to."

"Hi, Otto!" Stella hollered, running towards them. "Hi, Lizzie!"

"Hey, Stella. Where's everyone else?"

"They're looking at Buzz Calloway's project." She rolled her eyes. "Only because Hazel thinks Buzz is cute. His project is about dirt, which is *so* boring. Can I walk with you?"

"Sure thing, Squirt," Otto said. "Hey, let's go over there. Margaret is giving a demonstration of the radio she made."

"Ladies and Gentlemen, please find a seat. We will be announcing the winners momentarily. Thank you." Mr. Jackson stepped away from the microphone on the stage.

"I didn't know your uncle was emceeing for the fair," Otto told Lizzie as they went to find seats. Stella skipped along next to him.

"He did it a few years ago, too." Lizzie gestured to one of the rows of metal folding chairs. "Shall we sit here?"

They sat down while Mr. Jackson stepped back up to the microphone. "Ladies and Gentlemen, welcome to the twenty-ninth annual Dr. Spencer Newman Science Fair!" The crowd cheered for the chemist who'd grown up in Bayside and made it semi-famous.

Mr. Jackson introduced the five judges. Two were teachers from the high school, one was from the research institute started by Dr. Newman, and the last two, Dr. Winkler and his colleague, were from Oak Ridge.

"And now, the moment you've all been waiting for. We saw so many wonderful projects. You can all be proud of the boys and girls who put so much work into them."

Everyone whooped and hollered. Otto's jaw tightened as he joined the applause. His leg bounced up and down when the room quieted and Mr. Jackson announced the runners-up; Winston Avery, Max Booth, and... Milton Hayes?

Otto couldn't believe his ears. If Milton's project wasn't good enough, his definitely wasn't. He blew out a breath and sat back in his chair. Well, so much for that.

"And now, our winners!" Mr. Jackson made a show of adjusting his bow tie and opening an envelope. He drew out a slip of paper. "In third place, with a unique compilation of Lake Michigan's rocks and minerals... Otto Edwards!"

As the crowd erupted, Otto blinked. Him?

"Go, Otto!" Stella hissed.

"Get up!" Lizzie prodded him with her finger. "They're waiting."

Straightening his blue and white sport coat, Otto stood as Stella cheered and Lizzie let out a shrill whistle.

"That's my son!" Dad hollered from the back.

"Congratulations, Otto." Mr. Jackson shook his hand and gave him a white ribbon. "Go ahead and stay up here. We'll take a photo at the end."

"Thank you, sir." Otto grinned. His project had beaten *Milton's*.

The judges lined up to shake hands with him while Mr. Jackson announced the other winners.

"In second place, with a homemade radio and an explanation of radio waves and frequencies... Miss Margaret Woods!" More cheering chased Margaret up to the stage where she accepted her red ribbon, beaming proudly.

"And in first place, with an elaborate study in genetics by way of—ahem—hamster breeding... Ansel Donnelly!"

Ansel's many brothers raised a ruckus as the small boy with large glasses took the blue ribbon, a grin big enough to reach across the lake to Wisconsin stretched across his face.

A man from the newspaper had the winners pose with the judges, the camera flashing brightly. Congratulations came from all sides as everyone greeted the winners, but finally, things wound down as the science fair came to an end. People started taking down their projects and carrying them out of the gymnasium.

"Good job, Otto," Dad said, slapping his shoulder.

Mom gave him a peck on the cheek. "We're so proud of you."

"I told you the blue and white plaid makes you look smart," Hazel exclaimed with a smug look as Stella squeezed Otto tightly.

"Ready to head home?" Dad asked.

Otto glanced over at Lizzie, who was congratulating Margaret. "Actually, can I meet you at home later?"

Stella gasped. "Are you going to ask Lizzie on a date?" The last word barely squeaked out past her silly grin.

Otto could feel the heat rising in his face. "Well, maybe."

"I think it's time for us to go," Mom said. "Hazel, grab Otto's rocks and Paul, will you grab the display board?"

"Good luck, son." Dad winked and tilted his head toward Lizzie. As they left the gymnasium, Lizzie headed his way.

"I knew you could do it, Otto! Can I see your ribbon?"

"Sure." He handed the silky white ribbon to her. A gold "3" sat in the middle of the twin-tailed rosette. "Pretty neat, huh?"

"I love it. You should frame it." She gave it back. "So, what will you do to celebrate?"

Otto fidgeted with the button on his sleeve. "Well... I was wondering if you'd like to get root beer floats with me?"

Lizzie's eyes lit up, and she grinned. "Let me check with my parents. I'll be right back!"

"Excuse me," said a man in a gray pinstripe suit as Lizzie skipped away, "are you Otto Edwards?"

"Yes, sir. You're Dr. Winkler, the geology professor at Oak Ridge. You were one of the judges."

"Ah, very good." Dr. Winkler smiled. "I'm putting together a group of students to work on a geological survey of the area this summer. We would welcome the addition of someone like yourself. Here's my card. I don't need an answer now. But give me a call next week and let me know what you decide." He glanced at his watch. "Congratulations on your win, Mr. Edwards." He shook Otto's hand then hurried outside.

Lizzie ran over. "They said yes, but I have to be home by four. Ooh, what's that?" she asked as they stepped outside.

"Dr. Winkler gave it to me. He invited me to join him for a geological survey this summer."

"How exciting! Will you go?"

Otto studied Dr. Winkler's card. He had longed for this opportunity, and he would certainly learn a lot. He looked up at Lizzie, who was changing back into her Keds. A geological survey or...

What if he spent the summer beachcombing instead?

"I don't know. We'll see."

Pocketing the card, he thought of Hazel who loved him in her own weird way. And Stella who always wanted to tag along. They'd love to go beachcombing. What if he spent the summer with his sisters and... with Lizzie?

Lizzie shot a grin over her shoulder as she set her feet to the pedals of her yellow bike and sped down the sidewalk. Taking off his jacket and stuffing it in the saddlebag, Otto mounted his borrowed bike and took off after her.

A summer with Lizzie didn't sound bad at all. In fact, a summer with the girl who gave him a whole new perspective might be just what he needed

MEGAN WALTERS

Megan Walters has a chronic case of nostalgia which began her journey into the world of historical fiction, where it continued in the form of stacks of library books and late night rants about their accuracy. She hopes to honor the legacy of those who have gone before by inspiring readers to look into the past and find truths for the future. Megan has two cats and makes her home at the Crossroads of America, where she cracks herself up by telling her siblings bad jokes.

Achievements

- Drafted five projects including a novel and novella.

- Received two professional edit letters and implemented novel edits.

- Started a small product-based business in 2024.

- Attended Write-to-Publish and Author Conservatory pre-conference in 2024.

- Attended The Author Conservatory Conference in 2025.

- Attended the 2025 StorySell social media marketing workshop.

Pitches

- *Yours is the Night* meets *Gunner's Run* in a WWII historical about a young German woman who saves a downed American pilot in the hopes that he can help her find her MIA brother.

- *Seven Brides for Seven Brothers* meets *Short-Straw Bride* in a post-WWII historical about a cowboy with a mortgage to pay, siblings to raise, and the marriage of convenience that begins the healing his heart so desperately needs.

Like a Child
Nicole Elsierose

December 22, 1857

The day Marie Desmere had been waiting for ever since Mama had taught her how to count—her eighteenth—had arrived.

Beneath her quilted blanket, she shivered, although she doubted it was from the cold. Pulling the covers over her head, she closed her eyes, not quite ready to face her birthday without Papa.

The Papa who could lighten her mood simply with his warm smile and the deep husk of his voice. Something about his steady presence always took her back to the days of her youth when she fit snug in his strong arms, head perfectly held in the crook of his neck.

He was the very essence of nostalgia.

At least Papa would be back in time for Christmas.

"Marieee!"

She poked her head out of the blanket when the wood door burst open, and three curly-haired brunettes scampered into her bedroom. Their cheeks were flushed with cheerful warmth, blue eyes bright as the cold winter sky. Violet came first, the oldest of the three, charging forward in somewhat of an attempt to be ladylike as she held the side of her white frock dress. Gliding to the corner of Marie's rosewood bed, Violet wrapped her arms around Marie's neck, giving her a quick peck on the cheek.

"Happy birthday, Ree!"

"Thank—umph."

Two more sets of arms squeezed her tight. Her breath caught, words lost in the bundles of love. Seven, five, and three years old, all wrapped up in the embrace of Violet, Millie, and Ella.

She couldn't help smiling as they slid under her covers. Their tiny bodies fit so perfectly beside her, their heads resting on her shoulders. She pulled the quilt tighter around them, tucking them within her arms. Her eyes shut, soaking in the moment while it lasted.

They wouldn't be young forever.

Look at her—one moment she was being carried in Mama's arms as a toddler, Papa tucking her into bed with a breathtaking bedtime tale, his baritone voice rising and dipping and sliding into a mixture of different snowman characters he'd mimic, his exaggerated movements and wiggling eyebrows setting her off into endless giggles. It all seemed like *just* yesterday. Yet womanhood arrived quicker than she imagined, childhood slipping through her fingers.

More responsibilities, less frivolity.

Would this Christmas even feel the same?

Her gaze flitted to Mama's decorations. Furry garlands lined the mantle of the fireplace in her room, adorned with pinecones. A couple of paper snowflakes lay scattered across the room, matching the delicate beauty of the fluttering lace curtains and rose-patterned wallpaper. Her chestnut-colored writing desk sat by the large window, covered in books and drawing pencils, complete with her ink and quill pen—a gift from Papa last Christmas.

Her breath caught, and she glanced at her sleeping sisters beside her.

Their *gifts*... Papa would only be home late Christmas Eve, with hardly a moment to gather any presents; selling cattle throughout the Carolinas took days, and then came the travel time back to their home in Tennessee. Mama had her hands full with meals and last-minute preparations. And with tighter finances these past couple months, Marie knew well enough her sisters' presents would have to be handmade instead of bought.

Which meant only *she* could make them.

"Happy birthday, my sweet."

She turned her attention to Mama who stood by the door, her silky skirts billowing in their petticoated fashion. A smile tugged at Mama's lips as her eyes landed on the foursome snuggled on the bed, the younger three drifting off to a dreamy slumber.

Marie met Mama's gentle gaze, lowering her voice to a whisper. "Thank you, Mama. I love you so."

"And I, you."

A peaceful silence settled in the room as Mama placed fresh logs into the fireplace, lighting a small flame. Warmth floated through the room, washing over her face and chilled nose. Marie let out a soft sigh, leaning into the sleeping littles beside her.

A gentle smile touched Mama's face as she stepped closer. After opening the curtains, she took a seat on the bed by Marie's feet. Her gaze drifted beyond the window and onto the bright blue skies stretching across like a canvas and dipping into the patches of fields below.

"It's beautiful, isn't it?"

"Quite." Marie nodded. "Though, I suppose if we want a white Christmas, the skies will have to change colors."

"We've got time, we've got time..." Mama gave a small laugh. "Imagine your father's face if he arrives to his first white Christmas since our wedding year."

"It'd be quite the pleasant gift," Marie grinned. *Just like the gifts I'll surprise my sisters with. Something that can capture their childlike essence for them to keep forever.*

Ideas were already stirring.

"You think we should wake them?" Mama turned, a sparkle in her hazel eyes. "It *is* the day to decorate our tree..."

"Decorate?" Millie immediately sat up in bed, jolting her other sisters awake. "Ella, Vi! We're decorating today! Today is the *day*!"

Marie chuckled alongside Mama, sharing a knowing look. "That'll do it."

"Right there is perfect," Mama waved her arm, motioning to Eddie who stood by the front door. The young man of nineteen—and Marie's childhood friend—rolled the nine-foot pine tree in his wheelbarrow, the outdoor chill chasing him in as the wind slammed the door shut.

Marie stood by the side of the fireplace, carrying Ella in one arm. She wrapped her other arm around Millie and Violet while they watched with wide eyes.

A small curl of Eddie's brown hair fell across his forehead as he unloaded the tree in the opposite corner of the fireplace. His dark green vest and brown trousers matched the furry boughs and tree trunk. Wafts of pine swirled across the room, taking her back to her first Christmas memory: around four years old, watching Papa cut down a tree in their farmyard, whistling a merry tune while Mama scooped her up and tugged a wool bonnet to cover her tiny ears against the *thud* of the falling tree. But she hadn't been afraid of the noise, seeing her parents calm and cheery, singing and laughing as the tree came down and Papa lugged it home. There was a safeness in being little.

"Are the girls going to help decorate or watch me do all the hard work myself?"

Her sisters chuckled alongside Eddie as Marie gave a small smile.

Their gazes met, and a hint of concern flickered in his sparkling brown eyes.

Did he know how it ached to grow up? How, even though she'd always felt older than her age, childhood had been at her fingertips anytime she wanted to return to the safety of its embrace. But turning eighteen... the thought alone seemed to be the final closed door to any semblance of childhood.

Her sisters would have to face the same reality all too soon.

She blinked, breaking their gaze. Eddie's lingered for a moment more before turning to Mama and offering a hand to help carry the box of popcorn garland she had finished stringing the night before.

"Ree, Ree." Ella tugged at Marie's puffed sleeve. "I wanna 'corate too."

"Why, of course." Marie lowered the toddler to the wool carpet in the center of the parlor.

Ella scampered to her sisters who were gathered around Mama and Eddie. The parlor soon became filled with a flurry of ornaments: paper snowflakes, cranberry sprigs, and dried orange slices. The warm glow of the fireplace reflected in the pieces of silver tinsel Papa had gifted them years ago.

Marie took a step away, purpose beginning to pound through her veins.

She'd have to get started right away if she wanted to finish their present in time for Christmas in three days. Her fingers brushed past the oak wingback chair where Papa usually sat with the girls after dinner to recount stories and family lore. A smile tugged at her lips as she kept her footsteps light, reaching the polished wooden staircase.

"What are you doing?"

She blinked, turning to see Violet's bright face peeking behind the other side of the banister. *How'd she get here?*

"I'm going upstairs for a little while."

"Upstairs?" Violet's eyes grew wide.

"Just up to my room." Marie nodded, trying to maintain an even tone.

"Why are you whispering?"

"I am not." Marie's brows lifted, amusement tugging at her lips.

"Yes, you are! Do you have a secret? Perhaps—"

"Vi, why don't you help decorate?"

"But I wanted *you* to join us."

"I'm sorry…" A small sigh escaped Marie's lips, but she pressed another smile on. "When you get older, you just can't do everything you want to. You now have larger responsibilities."

"Oh yes." Violet nodded her head with an air of sophistication. "The big 'R' word. I know all about that."

Marie smirked. "Really…? Then why don't you take responsibility and help your sisters? You *are* the eldest among them, you know."

Violet's grin grew till she finally hurried away from the staircase and back to the group.

Marie held her skirts and traveled up the creaky stairs. Laughter floated up from the parlor below. Millie giggled the loudest, as she always did, but this time it seemed to flow so naturally alongside the rest of them. As if it were a melody all on its own. A tune so free and pure and childlike, unclouded by worry.

Her heart tugged, caught between wanting to rush back down to join them and desiring to bottle up their laughter in the gift she'd make. The latter won out when she reached the top of the stairs. Heading across the hallway and into her bedroom, she picked up the logs Mama had left her, quickly rekindling the embers. She stoked them till the flame was large enough to bring the needed warmth.

Pinning her curls back, she sat in her wicker rocking chair by the lace-covered window. She opened her desk drawer, taking out a leather-bound sketchbook that lay stacked atop numerous others and placing it on the table. Excitement pulsed through her fingers as she opened the book and traced her fingertips on a blank page.

Papa was always telling her how beautiful her art was, how she could so accurately capture a moment in time when words failed.

Now she'd do the same for her sisters. Drawings of memories made together, collecting each one to preserve for them for years to come.

Hour upon hour, Marie's fingers curved around her wooden pencil as it danced across the smooth paper, spinning memories and moments into markings. Portraits first: Ella's squishy cheeks, Millie's mischievous grin, and Violet's graceful posture trying to walk in her older sister's shoes.

She couldn't spare them from growing up, but she could slow time in her sketchbook.

Experience had taught her so. Each time they saw her working on a drawing of nature or daily life, they'd beg her to flip through the pages over and over again. Whimsy alight, wonder seeping from their every gasp. She savored the memories, pencil posed, ready to include them in her drawings.

But before she could continue, tendrils of cinnamon and butter swirled through the crack in her bedroom door, making her mouth water. She breathed in deeply.

Mama's cookies... Marie just couldn't resist.

Leaving her sketchbook on the rocking chair, she quietly crept out of her room and down the stairs. Evening light streamed from the windows, illuminating the large tree. Velvet ribbons dotted the furry boughs. They matched the tartan bows and pinecones hanging in an arranged bouquet that draped upon the metal curves of the wall sconces.

Marie quickened her pace to the kitchen.

An elegant lace tablecloth covered the long dining table, an evergreen garland stretching across the center. Red and green tartan ribbons tied to the backs of the wooden chairs completed the look. The ivory plates were already set, and on the far edge of the table sat a large plate of steaming cinnamon caraway cookies. Waiting just for her.

Her skirts brushed past the chairs as she made her way to the plate, taking a warm cookie in her fingers. She cupped her hand beneath her chin, careful not to drop any crumbs onto her dress. The soft cookie melted in her mouth and the toasted caraway seeds resembled an almost candy cane texture, reminiscent of when she was eight and Papa came home one day with her very first candy cane. All white, all sugar, and all smiles.

Every day leading up to Christmas that year, he hid one of those white canes all throughout the house for her to find, and each time she found one, he'd scoop her up in his arms with his grizzly laugh as she reached for a high tree branch to place the canes on.

A decade of growing up left those days long buried.

Hearing Mama's footsteps approaching, Marie quickly stuffed the rest of the cookie into her mouth as gracefully as she could. She exited the dining room and headed up the stairs once more.

Girlish giggles beckoned her past her bedroom to the room her sisters shared. The door stood slightly ajar.

Peeking in, she caught the threesome sitting on the carpet, huddled around a large woven basket. *Her* childhood basket. Baby books and small toys were strewn around them.

Ella and Millie gathered close to Violet, peering over her shoulder as she dug her hands deeper into the basket.

"I found something else!" She squealed, lifting a bulky cloth with surprising gentleness before setting it in front of her sisters. Beaming, Violet unwrapped the cloth, and Ella's eyes sparkled as she grabbed Millie's arm, as if awaiting what other wonders they'd just discovered.

But their smiles quickly vanished, replaced by horrified gasps as Violet lifted a porcelain doll, her once beautifully hand-painted face now cracked.

Marie held back her own gasp. Her eyes trailed the long ugly splinters running across the doll's forehead that led to her shattered skull and chipped nose. She hadn't opened the basket since their move three years earlier... the doll must've not been packed as safely as she'd thought.

"Oh," Ella whispered, her tiny shoulders sagging.

A heavy silence hung in the air, wringing through Marie's heart.

Papa's gift to me when I was ten, my favorite doll. Another piece of my childhood, gone. I can't allow that to happen to them.

The battered doll stared back at her, urging her to return to her drawing before her sisters could see her.

"Marie..."

"Marie, wake up..."

Her shoulders shook, Mama's voice close to her ear.

Marie sat up, rubbing her eyes against dawn's light breaking loose from her lace curtains. "Whatever is the matter?" Her gaze fell upon Ella in Mama's arms, her tiny cheeks rosy.

Mama's brows dipped. "I woke to find Ella with a small cold. Doctor Elias came over from visiting Mrs. Greyson next door. Her ankle is healing quite nicely. As for Ella, it's nothing contagious, thank the good Lord. Likely just from the colder weather."

"Oh." Relief mingled with compassion, and Marie reached out a hand to stroke Ella's cheek, listening to Mama tell of how she'd been up with Ella all morning, wrapping the little one in a warm blanket by the fireplace.

"It should pass within a day or two." Mama nodded, her eyes softening. "But I thought you could help me take care of her as I ride to town for some fresh meat to make a nice warm soup for her. I should be back by supper."

"That's all right." Marie threw her quilt to the side and climbed out of bed to dress in her everyday petticoat, cotton dress, and shawl.

She fingered through her tousled brunette ringlets, then held out her arms to receive the little one, holding her close. Ella's cheek lay perfectly upon Marie's bosom, right near her heart.

There was nearly nothing in the world Marie enjoyed more than holding a child in her arms. The feeling caressed her soul, stirring up a certain warmth as if she'd been made for it.

Gazing into Ella's petite face, she pressed a kiss on her forehead.

She could feel Mama's smile and a rush of nostalgia, as if she was thinking of when Marie was Ella's age. How the time flew by...

"Thank you, Ree."

Marie nodded, slowly rocking Ella side to side as she shuffled her feet across the rug.

"Oh, Marie," Mama spoke up again, "Could you also spend some time with Millie and Vi today... They're down a playmate and feeling quite glum."

"Yes, of course." Marie nodded, but inside, a twinge of worry nipped at her. She could've gotten away with Ella asleep, but with the two other girls, she couldn't work on their gift. If they even caught a glimpse of her pencils, they'd clamor to see what she was working on, and the surprise would be ruined.

"Thank you, dear," Mama said again, wrapping her arms around her. "I knew I could count on you. I'll bring you breakfast in a few minutes."

Marie nodded absently, thinking about the moment she could return to her sketchbook, be it that tomorrow was Christmas Eve. Ella stirred in her arms, and Marie's gaze flickered to the sleeping toddler.

Today was still a gift, wasn't it?

Holding one of God's blessings in her arms made it so.

Mama's footsteps faded down the stairs, and Marie followed, quietly making her way down the long hall.

Fluffy garland lined the wooden banister, and a dozen silver bells rang like fairy laughs below. At least, that's what she'd always thought they sounded like when she was younger.

Tearing her gaze from the staircase, she stepped across the hall and gave a small knock upon her sisters' bedroom before entering.

Two pairs of blue eyes brightened as the girls leapt up from the wooden rocking horses Papa had handcrafted a few years back.

Carefully, Marie set Ella on the bed Millie and Violet shared. She pulled the covers atop, brushing curls out of the little one's face. Turning her attention to the girls, she came over to them by the large window seat that overlooked the field outside their home. The sky had turned an odd shade of white, like a blanket of vanilla frosting.

"Do you think it's going to snow?" Violet whispered.

"I was going to ask the same thing." Marie gave a quiet laugh. "Do you *want* it to snow?"

"Yes! Oh yes!" Millie clapped her hands together, eyes alight.

Marie smiled but held a finger to her lips. "Try to keep it quiet for Ella... we want her to rest, alright?"

The girls nodded solemnly.

"You really think she's going to be okay?" Violet asked, biting her lip.

"Of course she is." Marie wrapped an arm around them both, gently pulling them close. "God is taking care of Ella. There's nothing to worry about."

"Baby Jesus?" Millie whispered. "Like the Nativity set Mama has downstairs?"

"Something like that..." Marie's lips lifted into a small grin. "Only now baby Jesus is grown and a good friend to us. He loves us very much."

"Like Papa." Violet nodded, tilting her head to rest it upon Marie's shoulder.

"Like Papa." Marie nodded back. "Yet somehow loving us a million times more."

A peaceful silence drifted upon them like delicate snowflakes. Marie eyed Ella's sleeping form on the bed, smiling to see her chest gently rise and fall with restful breaths.

"Ree." Millie gave a small tug on her sleeve.

"Mm."

"Why don't you ever play with us anymore?"

Marie blinked. "What... do you mean?"

"Yes." Violet nodded, blue eyes peering up at her. "If you see us play, you only watch us. As if you're making sure we're staying out of trouble."

Marie's eyebrows raised. "Well, it's not *quite* like that. I know you are good girls and stay away from mischief."

"Then why don't you join us?" Violet prodded. "You seemed to have stopped ages ago."

Marie remembered how at sixteen, playing with the girls became less and less till she stopped altogether. She'd felt a strange emptiness anytime she tried to force herself to go along with the girls as they bounced up and down with their rolling hoops, pretending they were in a horse race. Or when their marbles became food for their paper dolls to have during teatime.

"Ree?"

She gave a small shake of her head. "I..."

"It's 'cause you grew up, isn't it?" Violet tilted her head, her voice softening.

Seven and too young to come to such a conclusion, even if there *was* truth to it.

Marie looked away, her gaze traveling to the bed. "I think I'll check up on Ella for a minute."

She stood quickly, stepping close to the bedside to feel Ella's cheeks, which were much cooler already.

But Violet's words still echoed in her mind.

At last, Mama had come home, and the day wore into the evening.

Marie kissed the girls goodnight, then quietly tiptoed to her room. Memories fresh on her mind, she poured them through her fingers, watching the drawings take shape just like how her mind remembered them.

Her sisters at play, heads tilted back in sweet laughter, the precious sound caught in the pages, refined with her pencil till she could almost hear them twinkling like the fairy—*silver*—bells downstairs. She dared to draw those next, then Mama decorating the table, and Papa making funny faces to make Ella laugh, Millie's gleaming eyes as she snuck one of Mama's cookies, and Violet dancing across the wood floors of their kitchen while Mama stirred supper on the stove. Spring picnics and Papa's fiddle-playing during breezy summer nights while the girls chased fireflies till the melody grew tender with the evening, Ella drifting off to sleep in Mama's arms while Millie and Violet leaned their heads on Marie's shoulders.

Long into the night, she drew every ounce of childhood her sisters had experienced thus far, working under the flickering candlelight till her heart had poured out everything it could offer.

She blew out the flame before climbing into bed.

It seemed only a minute since her eyes shut before the light peeked through the handiwork of the lace curtains and stirred her awake once more.

As she dressed herself in layers, her gaze drifted to the finished sketchbook. All but one page had been filled, the final drawing to be completed when Papa arrived and they celebrated Christmas together tomorrow.

Then she'd start another sketchbook, one for each year.

For now, the only thing missing was some of that pretty paper Papa always wrapped their presents with.

Which meant a quick visit to Eddie, who happened to be the nephew of the Mercantile's manager. If anyone had wrapping paper this late in the season, it was Eddie.

She swept a shawl over her shoulders, grabbed mittens, and slipped into her winter boots before heading down the long winding staircase and out the front door.

A blast of cold air met her, and her teeth began to chatter.

Perhaps Papa *would* get his white Christmas tomorrow.

Pulling the shawl tighter, Marie walked across the dirt pathway to Eddie's house across the street. Shivering, she gave a light *rap, tap, tap* on the door and waited, rubbing her mitten-laden hands together.

The tall wood door creaked opened, warmth seeping from inside.

"Ree." Two sparkling brown eyes met her in a nostalgic welcome.

"Ed," She returned with a smile, ducking under his arm as he held the door open for her.

"What brings you here on this fine, frigid day?" He grinned, swinging the door shut.

His red and black flannel vest caught her eye, another childhood memory tickling. But minus the small jest of nicknames, she reminded herself that her childhood was over. She was here for her sisters' childhoods now.

"You never answered my question." Eddie eased himself close to the hearth, leaning his elbows on the stone. "I know you've not come here to stare." He gave a small chuckle. "Though perhaps to draw another portrait of *someone* I know."

"Tsk." Marie couldn't help smiling. "You know I already got plenty. Just about every time you've come over for the last... ah..." She counted her fingers. "Nine years."

"All right, all right." He smirked. "What have you trekked all the way here for?"

"It's only across the street, silly," She shook her head. "But on a serious note, I wanted to ask if you had any extra wrapping paper. For my sisters' present."

"Ah, yes." Eddie nodded, leading her into the kitchen.

Voices drifted from upstairs, likely from his mother and younger brother. Sprigs of evergreen lined the house, tied with tartan ribbon and holly berries. Stockings hung from the fireplace, waiting to be stuffed with little trinkets from his uncle's shop.

Eddie paused beside a large wood cabinet near their dining table, opening the ornately carved doors that held a mixture of plates, cups, and drawers of odds and ends from the shop.

"What are you gifting them anyway?" He dug his hands into the drawers.

"A sketchbook."

"Sketchbook?" He pulled out a rectangle-sized floral-patterned paper and a string of twine. "This good? It's all I have, I'm afraid. The shop's sold out except for this."

"Looks just about the right size." Marie took the paper and twine from his outstretched hand. "But wait... what about your presents?"

"Already wrapped. Anyways, Ben's growing older. Fourteen, that lad. He's not wanting much anymore, except a pleasant day with family. He says he's outgrowing presents."

"Sounds... mature." Marie's brows raised. "He should enjoy it more, these childhood Christmases. Not be in such a hurry to grow."

"I'm sure he's fine." Eddie gave a small shrug. "Besides, don't we all just carry bits and pieces of our childhood into years beyond, the memories stacking up into a lifetime of a masterpiece? Like all your sketchbooks combined?"

Marie was quiet for a moment. "I suppose. Or it could just be that you're getting poetic on me again... you really should take that up, you know."

He gave a small smile. "Really. Give it some thought. Perhaps you'll find it again."

If only it were that simple.

Marie leaned forward, her fingers tucking the sketchbook inside the paper on her desk. Once they unwrapped it tomorrow, she'd draw their Christmas day on the last page.

Excitement fluttered in her chest as she reached for the long strands of twine to tie the package together.

One, two, three times, she wrapped it around, bringing it to the center for a final knot. Taking the two ends, she completed the ribbon with a tug and—

"What are you doing?"

Marie jumped, her nails snagging the paper. It ripped into a long tear.

The package began unraveling faster than she could stop it. With wide eyes, the broken paper drifted to the floor, leaving the sketchbook bare in her hands.

Ella stared back at her.

Marie quickly slid the sketchbook behind her back, hoping, praying Ella didn't see it too clearly.

"For me?" Ella rubbed her sleepy eyes.

"You'll find out soon enough." She sighed, slipping the sketchbook into a drawer and standing to gather Ella in her arms. The corner of Marie's eye caught the torn paper on the ground. She frowned. *Papa always had things wrapped in my childhood...*

"Marie." Mama's voice sounded muffled behind the door. "Could I see you for a moment?"

Balancing Ella on her hip, her layered skirts shifted as she made her way to the door. Shutting it behind her, she found Mama leaning on the garland-laden staircase, wiping her cheeks. Marie drew in a breath, eyes tracing Mama's tear stains and the crease between her brows.

"Ree." Mama nodded at Ella, tilting her head in the direction of her sisters' room.

Despite her rising nerves, Marie pressed a smile, trying to make her voice light for the youngest one. "Ella, how about you play with Vi and Millie? Perhaps they'll do your favorite hoop game."

She rounded the hall as Ella giggled. "Yes, hoops!"

Once in the sisters' room, they quickly became distracted with their game.

Marie slipped away and back to Mama.

"What's wrong?" Marie tugged on a stray curl, swiping her hair back to meet Mama's gaze.

"It looks like your father won't be coming home tonight."

Marie drew in a sharp breath. "Why not?"

"The newsboy came to deliver the paper and said that a heavy snowstorm is traveling across the Carolinas, soon to arrive to our town." Mama let out a sigh. "It's expected to last for days."

"Days?" Marie echoed, her head spinning. "But Christmas is *tomorrow*."

"I know, dear," Mama put her arm around Marie, drawing her close.

Laughter came tumbling from her sisters' bedroom, echoing down the hall. That kind of childlikeness seemed further from her than ever.

"Let's not tell them till the last second." Mama's voice was low, but a faint spark of hope still shone through. "For all we know, a miracle is on the way."

If only Marie could believe, too.

Marie sat by her bedroom window, sketchbook open on her lap.

Flurries of snowflakes hurried by the glass pane, swirling onto the ground below. Already, she could barely recognize the once-grassy field, now covered in powdery layers.

She glanced at her sketchbook and the last blank page awaiting to be filled tomorrow.

The drawing wouldn't be the same without Papa.

Would her sisters still be smiling for their portraits? Or would the drawings be filled with frowns because he's not home?

A knock at the door made her jump. She quickly hid the sketchbook under a nearby shawl.

"Ree," Millie called, and Violet's voice echoed beside her.

"Come in, girls."

Millie pushed the door open, her petite frame bouncing into the room, eyes sparkling. Violet trailed behind her.

Millie's words came out in one long breath. "Guess what! Mama said me and Ella and Vi could go outside and play in the snow, and we can make snowmen and everything! And then Mama's making hot chocolate and cookies, and,

and..." She huffed a breath.

Violet patted her sister's shoulder, giggling. "Millie, slow down."

"Sounds like an adventure." Marie lifted a small smile.

Millie's energy rivaled the way she used to be.

"Oh, and"—Millie stretched out her hand—"can you play with us? Just this once?"

Violet glanced at Marie, offering a smile, "That is, *if* you still like snowmen."

Memories fluttered into her mind: Papa's bedtime stories about silly snowmen coming alive on Christmas Eve, dancing, laughing, and playing in the snow.

And before Papa or Mama or Marie ever knew her sisters would be born, Papa told sweet tales about a snowman family and four sisters, just like them. Her blessings.

Marie's lips curved into a grin. "Snowmen were one of my *favorite* parts of Christmas."

"So you'll come?" Violet's smile widened, as if daring to hope.

Marie clasped her hand around Millie's outstretched one and stood. "Let's go."

Daylight's hours flew by as she helped her sisters roll balls of snow and stack them in trios, forming a snowman for each of them out in their backyard. Ella sat on the ground, mittens drawing circles in the snow. Marie laughed as Millie and Violet stood side by side, comparing their heights to the snowmen.

"Ree." Ella tugged at Marie's woolen skirt. "Can I get my carrots?"

Marie nodded, scooping Ella onto her hip. "Gladly. Mama should have some ready for us. Girls." She waved at Millie and Violet. "I'll be back in a minute."

Ice crunched underneath her boots as Marie stepped across the field and into the kitchen with Ella. "Mama? Do you have the—"

"Carrots?" Mama's head peeked from the dining room as she entered the kitchen with a small bundle in her hands. "They're on the counter. And these are coal pieces from Papa's storage."

Marie thanked Mama, receiving the bundle of coal in one mittened hand while balancing Ella on her hip. She neared the counter, tilting slightly so Ella could reach the carrots.

"My carrots!" Ella held them close to her coat, then blinked. "Well… I *guess* I could share. Snowmen should have a good Christmas, too."

Marie grinned as Mama kissed the top of Ella's curls. "That's my girl."

Once out the door, Marie lowered Ella, and the younger ran ahead, carrots in hand. Marie glanced around the snowy field, eyes narrowing to catch a glimpse of Millie and Violet. "Where could they have—oof!"

A snowball pelted her shoulder.

She spun around, spying the girls hiding behind a tree trunk. Its branches were bare, but the trunk was large enough to cover them.

They locked eyes with her, blue on blue gleaming.

"Oh, it's on now." She dropped the bundle of coal, bending to gather a snowball in her mittens.

The girls dashed from behind the tree, and Marie ran to catch up.

"Don't hit me!" Ella giggled beside the snowmen, shaking her carrots in the air.

Squeals and laughter drifted through the yard as Marie chased her two sisters around Ella, up to the house door, back down and around.

A rare joy bloomed in her chest, and Eddie's words came whirling back to her.

Perhaps I didn't lose my childhood after all. It was only tucked deep inside, waiting for a moment like this.

The afternoon swirled past them. Heads tilting back, tongues sticking out to catch snowflakes. Hands grasping hands as they spun in circles before plopping onto the fluffy snow, spreading their arms into angel wings. And, as they placed the final touches on their snowmen, the snowfall slowed to a stop.

"Girls, hot chocolate and cookies!"

Within seconds, they skidded across the field and into the foyer, quickly peeling off their boots before they entered the living room. The candles on the tree had been lit, as was the grand fireplace, creating a warm glow throughout the dim house.

By the glistening pine tree, Mama greeted them with a silver tray of cookies and rosy pink teacups of cocoa. Marie grinned as the younger girls clapped their hands and bounced up and down.

She guided her sisters to the couch, and they immediately began munching. Even Mama lowered herself onto the armchair where Papa usually sat, taking a sip from her rosette teacup.

The fireplace crackled as they worked on their snacks. No one said much except for thanking Mama.

Marie sipped her cocoa as the girls wiped their sticky fingers on a lace napkin. She pulled a nearby blanket over them, and they snuggled close.

"This was the best day ever!" Millie exclaimed.

Mama smiled. "Why is that, my dear?"

"Because…" Violet glanced at her older sister. "Ree finally played with us."

"Is that so?" Mama's eyes twinkled when she looked at Marie.

"It was a good day," Marie agreed, leaning her head close to the girls. She couldn't wait to draw everything later and start a new sketchbook. But for now, she'd be present. Soak up all the childlikeness she could receive.

Evening's hours grew late into the night as the youngsters began to drift off. Marie caught Mama smiling at her.

"I'm proud of you, Ree." Mama's eyes shone. "I know you usually don't engage in such frivolity anymore."

"I suppose I needed it." Marie closed her eyes, savoring the afternoon's memories. "To see things from their eyes for a bit."

Mama nodded. "They're a gift to this world. As are you."

Thud, thud, thud…

Marie straightened. "Do you hear that?"

"Yes…" Mama whispered, eyeing the door.

A muffled voice echoed from behind it, growing more recognizable by the second.

"Is anyone home?"

Papa!

NICOLE ELSIEROSE

Nicole started her writing adventure in 1st grade, stapling together printer paper to create her own little booklets, but it wasn't until an 8th grade composition class that she realized writing would be more than something she did just for fun. Now, she blends historical and contemporary fiction to create stories of hope and heart that feel like home. When not writing, Nicole loves curling up with a mug of hot cocoa year round, listening to her favorite songs on repeat, and creating content for her Instagram—combining her love of dance, photography, and storytelling.

Achievements

- Grew her Instagram platform to 1k+ in 4 months.

- Published in *The Rebelution* at 15 years old.

- Sold over 20 handmade jewelry and accessories in the first three weeks of starting her first-ever Etsy shop.

- Has helped numerous authors (Anna Rose Johnson, Victoria Lynn, and more) in their street teams, ARC reading, and book reviews.

- Received a full manuscript assessment from a professional editor on her 60k word novel.

Pitches

- A YA contemporary about a high school senior teaming up with her bestie for a highly-acclaimed photography competition, but when her bestie has to move unexpectedly, she must navigate staying in touch while working alongside a brand new set of teammates - and finding them to be the friends she didn't know she needed.

- A Ginger Rogers/Fred Astaire inspired story about a tap dancer and wannabe author during the Great Depression who learns how broken dreams can be a gift after all.

CONTEMPORARY
Adult

Nibbles & Bytes
Lauren Thomae

C arson hated his life.

Sitting in his office chair, after adding a few more tweaks to this section of the spreadsheet, he'd be done for the night.

His burning eyes didn't want to finish it. They wanted to go home and go straight to bed, and without driving through St. Louis traffic first.

But his boss's words came back to him as he rubbed his forehead. "You could be the youngest person to ever get a promotion like this!" "This is quality work!" "I've never seen any new hire work as hard as you do!"

And a text from his dad, still clear in his mind. "Let me know how the presentation goes next week. Proud of you."

Carson could keep working for a while longer.

Carson stumbled out of the quiet office building to his lonely car in the middle of the empty parking lot. He wanted to feel proud that nobody else stayed as late as he did. And since college was only six months behind him, he considered that pretty good. But it was much harder to feel pride when his eyes felt ready to melt right out of his head.

He glanced at his phone. It showed three missed calls from his neighbor Betty and an alarming number of texts, asking him where he was. He'd forgotten dinner with Betty and her husband, yet again.

Thankful that landlords didn't kick out their tenants for missing dinner invitations, he sent her a quick apology text. He'd *meant* to make it tonight. Heck, he *wanted* to make it, but then he came so close to finishing up another piece of his marketing presentation. It was the one his boss, Tom, had specifically asked him to create highlighting the company's newest piece of tech. The one he would present in front of new clients. He just couldn't leave without finishing it. Not with Tom depending on him, and not with the thought of a promotion in the back of his mind.

Carson threw his laptop bag into the car, and an unusual sound reached his ears.

Meowing.

Not exactly a sound normally heard in a corporate parking lot. He peered down the alley separating the buildings. It soon got louder.

He took a couple cautious steps forward, until his foot bumped against something.

He looked down at his feet where a scrawny, dirt-streaked kitten wound around his ankle and meowed again. "Oh, hey!"

"What are you doing here, little guy?" Carson looked around for a mother cat, an owner, anything. But the kitten's cries only got louder as if insisting that he was all alone.

"Come here." Carson scooped up the kitten, holding it close to stop its shivering.

The kitten stopped crying, purred, and tried to bite the buttons on his shirt.

Carson glanced around again. Maybe if he stayed for just a little longer, the owner would magically appear, saying that they'd been looking for it all day, and Carson was a hero for finding it.

Unfortunately for both of them, no one came.

Carson stared down at the fluffball that could have blended into his black jacket, with the exception of its yellow eyes, and the dirt caked on its body. So much like his childhood cat, who in the same way, found Carson in a parking lot and screamed until he took him home. It even purred the same way, making muffled little meows in between the purrs.

But he really didn't have time to take care of this cat—as much as he wanted to. His focus needed to stay on the project and his promotion. He couldn't spare any time for distractions, especially in the shape of dirty little kittens.

Carson sighed and looked at the kitten now purring contentedly in his arms.

His million reasons for saying no ran through his mind, but he couldn't bring himself to put the cat down and leave it.

"I guess you're coming with me, little dude," he whispered to the kitten, setting it in the passenger's seat before climbing into the car. "But only because the shelters are closed right now. You're leaving first thing in the morning." Carson slid into the driver's seat and watched the kitten clamber over and curl up in his lap.

The only reason he was bringing the kitten home was because he was a nice person who didn't leave helpless kittens out in the cold. That was the only reason.

His phone buzzed. A text from his boss, wondering if he could come in earlier tomorrow.

Carson sighed again but texted back, "Absolutely!"

Pulling out of the parking lot, he wondered how early the shelters were open.

"If you would stop struggling for one second," Carson said, frowning at the kitten in his left hand and struggling to unlock the door with his right. "We could get inside."

If someone had told him this morning that managing to unlock his door without dropping a kitten would be his biggest achievement of the day, he might have laughed.

"Carson?" A voice called him from the other side of the porch, startling him so hard he did almost drop the kitten.

His neighbor, Betty, leaned out the door of her side of the duplex with curlers in her hair and slippers on her feet. "What have you got there?"

"Oh, hi!" He smiled and lifted up the kitten so she could see. "I found this little guy in the parking lot at the office, and it was too late to take him to a shelter. I didn't want to leave him there..." Carson's voice trailed off as he took in Betty's appearance. "I didn't wake you up, did I?"

Betty waved the worry off, grinning as she shuffled closer to see the kitten. "No, no, I just wanted to make sure you got home okay, after you missed dinner earlier." She took the kitten and held it close, still smiling. The kitten purred as if pleased to be held by someone who wasn't in such a hurry. "He's a sweetie! Were you able to get food and things for him?"

Carson squeezed his eyes shut. Kittens *needed* things, didn't they? Like food, litter, food bowls... "Oh no," he groaned, trying to rub away the sudden headache. "I didn't even think about that. I'll have to go and—"

"Nonsense." Betty headed back inside, waving at him to follow, kitten in hand. "Ed and I have a cat and have plenty of extra things. Let's save you from making a trip."

"There we go." Betty smiled, setting down the last of the toys.

Carson watched the kitten scramble around his living room, now filled with brightly colored kitten toys and supplies. "How often did you say I should feed it again?"

"Him. It's a him, not an 'it.'" Betty said. She smiled again as the kitten pattered back over to her. "You need to give him a name. I recommend feeding him twice a day and try to keep a close eye on him so he doesn't get into everything."

Carson nodded. He was thankful for all of Betty's help, but he wasn't going to name the kitten, because *he* was going to a shelter in the morning. He didn't have time for a pet. His open laptop with thirty unread work emails told him that much. But Betty was being so kind to him, even though he always missed her dinner invitations. "Hopefully he'll be all right. I won't be able to come home and check on him with everything going on at work."

Glancing at his laptop again, he debated about going through the emails before bed. His boss wouldn't accept taking care of a new kitten as an excuse for falling behind.

"Better put away anything you don't want him using as a toy." Betty said, but as he slid his laptop closer, his mind returned to the office. "I'd hate for you to come home and see that the little rascal broke something important."

Carson nodded, still attempting to smile politely as he clicked through the emails. Tom had already sent him some more adjustments to make. He made mental tweaks to his presentation as Betty continued to talk.

"Are you going to be all right?" she said, causing him to look up.

He closed the laptop, watching the kitten eat his food.

How much trouble could it really be?

"Yeah, I think we'll be fine. It's just for the night." He stood, stretched, and walked Betty to the door. "Thank you so much for everything. I really appreciate it."

"Would you like me to keep the kitten while you're at work tomorrow? Just in case it ends up being another late night?" Betty asked as she stepped outside.

Carson paused. He didn't want the kitten to still be here tomorrow night, but Betty was right. What if he ended up working late again? What if the shelters weren't open in the morning?

Pushing down the guilt he felt at accepting her kindness again, he said, "Yeah, that would be great actually. If you're sure."

"It's no trouble at all!" Betty grinned and waved as she crossed the porch, her slippers flopping as she went. "Just bring him over in the morning. With a name!"

The door clicked shut, saving Carson the trouble of answering. He breathed in the chilly night air while a kitten snuggled around his legs.

Pushing it gently back inside with his foot, he shut and locked the door behind him.

Carson shook himself as he settled into bed, turning his mind back to work. He couldn't afford to be distracted. Thankfully Betty would take care of the kitten, and he could work without worrying about it destroying his house—

Something crashed.

He jumped out of bed and burst back into the living room.

A lamp lay on the floor, thankfully unbroken, with the kitten nowhere to be found.

He sighed and rubbed his forehead. It was going to be a long night.

Carson knocked gently on the door, cringing at how late it was.

To be fair, it was *much* earlier than he normally came home.

It was practically still working hours for him, and his phone was buzzing with texts and emails. All from his boss.

Unfortunately, the shelters didn't open until he was at work, and they closed before he could get away. So Nibble—as he now called the bitey kitten—was still here.

Betty opened the door with a smile. "Come in! You're just in time." She led him to the cozy kitchen and pulled a tray of double chocolate chip cookies out of the oven.

The cookies threatened to fall apart as Betty eased them onto a cooling rack. Before Carson could protest, she slid a few onto a napkin and into his hands.

"I'll go gather up Nibble. He's had quite the day rampaging all over the house," Betty said, as Carson switched the hot cookies from hand to hand, trying not to drop them.

He watched her go and shook his head.

"She certainly wastes no time, does she?" Ed, Betty's husband and Carson's landlord, shuffled in, grabbed a cookie and popped it in his mouth. "I tell her that she could lighten up on the chocolate, but she pretends not to hear me." He sighed and winked at Carson, obviously not bothered in the slightest.

"Lots of late nights recently." Ed snatched another cookie. "Everything going okay at work?"

Carson laughed awkwardly and ran a hand through his hair. "Yeah, it's been pretty crazy lately. I have a huge presentation coming up next week."

And a promotion was sure to follow. *If* the presentation went well.

Ed nodded, his bushy eyebrows knit together in thought. "I remember those days well. Wouldn't say I miss them." He peered at Carson. "You fix computers, is that right?"

Carson hesitated. "Not really. I mean, that's what I'd like to do, but I work in the marketing department."

Ed's smile grew. "Would you mind looking at my computer? Something's got to be wrong with it, and I can't figure it out. I've been meaning to ask my son to look at it, but he hasn't been able to make it over."

Carson nodded. He liked working with computers. That's partially why he chose the name "Nibble," because a computer nibble was half of a byte. Ed's computer probably only needed a simple fix anyway. He and Betty had helped him out so much over the past few days, it was the least he could do. "Sure." He followed him into the office.

Carson blinked as he entered, widening his eyes to try and take everything in.

It was as if Ed was an amateur photographer, trying to cover every square inch of space with pictures, so much so that the pictures seemed to meld together into a wallpaper that covered every blank space. The only furniture was a roll-top desk shoved into the corner and two matching chairs.

Ed brought him to the desk, with the brand-new laptop nestled in the middle of mismatched picture frames. Carson hoped that nothing was *too* wrong with it.

"My son just got this for me, after the old one died." Ed said, settling into a chair and frowning at the laptop. "But I just can't seem to figure it out."

Carson opened it up and watched the monitor chime its welcome sequence. "Did he not set it up for you?"

"Set it up?"

Carson grinned as he sat in the other chair, his uneasiness leaving. *This* he could help with.

He plugged in all the needed information, even changed the welcome screen to a picture of Ed's family at his request. Normally he'd worry about the time he was losing on his presentation, but since it was so early, he managed not to think too much about it.

"Is this easier or harder than what you do at work?" Ed said, his eyes twinkling with good humor as they waited for all of the updates to be installed.

Carson sighed, leaning back in the chair until it squeaked. "It's definitely easier." He pulled away from the desk, watching the computer load. As the progress bar inched forward, he found his eyes wandering around the office.

Frames were stuffed behind and beside the computer, and everything from neatly framed portraits to blurry polaroids. School photos, people on camping trips, at bonfires, and during Christmas time. Even Pickle, their cat, had made the cut with a photo haphazardly taped onto the back of the door.

Carson stood and leaned closer to the photos on the wall before pointing at one of them. "Where was this one taken?"

Ed squinted at the photo before grinning. "In Alaska. We took the whole family to celebrate my retirement." He chuckled, sitting back in his chair. "I don't think we'll ever forget the view of those mountains, how they just kept on going up and up. It was certainly a welcome sight after all those years sitting at my desk."

Carson stopped at an ornately framed family portrait, obviously professionally taken. "How many kids do you have?"

"Three. And five grandkids, so far."

Carson didn't have pictures in his house. Or in his cubicle at work. Or on his phone even. The only pictures he had were of work notes, and one he took of Nibble on that first night.

"How did you have time for all of your family and these trips and everything?" Carson asked. He didn't even have time to call his dad back. "With working?"

Ed shrugged. "How could I not have time for it?" He scanned the room with a soft smile. "Nothing was better than coming home to see them."

Carson nodded, but a part of him didn't understand. He lived alone, and even if he didn't, he wouldn't have time for anyone.

Would his life ever look like Ed's?

The computer sang its little song, letting them know that the updates were done.

Carson returned to his chair and typed in the last few commands. He stared at the picture of Ed and his family for another second before standing up.

Ed clapped him on the back, thanking him profusely as they left the office.

"Were you able to get everything figured out?" Betty entered the hallway, Nibble held in one hand and a container of cookies in the other. "Thank you so much for doing that. Ed's been tinkering with it for days."

"I would have gotten it eventually!" Ed held a hand to his chest as if to look offended, but his grin ruined the effect.

Carson took the squirming kitten and container of goodies. He thanked her and headed toward the door.

"We were thinking that since tomorrow is the six-month anniversary of you being our neighbor," Betty said as she brushed her hand on her apron. "We could all go out to breakfast tomorrow! How does that sound? We'd be happy to treat you, and since it's Saturday, you won't have to work!"

Six months? Already?

He set the container down on the hallway table, petting Nibble. Just like every other Saturday he planned on working. The presentation was due on Monday, and he needed to fix so much before then.

His phone buzzed.

It was a text from his sister Maisie, wishing him good luck on the presentation.

He could imagine her rolling her eyes at the thought of him working on a Saturday and how she would push him to go to breakfast instead.

But the presentation was on *Monday*, not Saturday or Sunday.

He could spare a few hours for breakfast tomorrow, especially for these people who were so generous toward him.

"Sure, I'd love to do that." Carson smiled as Betty clapped her hands in excitement.

"We'll see you in the morning then." Ed opened the door so Carson could leave with both the kitten and the cookies.

Carson held up the kitten in farewell and walked back home.

He set the kitten on the couch before dropping next to it. He opened the container and shoved a cookie in his mouth. Whatever Ed had said, Carson thought Betty had used the perfect amount of chocolate.

Keeping the container away from the kitten's curious paws, he grabbed another cookie. He wasn't going to cook dinner anyway, and his mom wasn't around to scold him for filling up on cookies.

Carson squinted at the far wall, empty except for the TV his dad had helped him install when he first moved in. His mom had cleaned the place that day, wiping out drawers and other things he didn't think about. She would've spent ridiculous amounts of money on decorations if he'd let her. He then sent them all home after they helped him unpack, insisting that he was on his own now and could handle things.

But the white walls seemed to mock him, and he could almost hear Maisie making fun of the spectacular job he had done. There truly wasn't an ounce of personality in sight. No pictures, no posters, nothing. Just his work laptop and more scribbled notes than six months of work should have produced.

Laughter from next door made his chest feel heavy and light at the same time. Ed and Betty were the only people he'd really connected with since moving. *Actually* connected with, not in a professional co-worker way, but in a way that made him feel like a part of their family.

And he'd only learned tonight that they had kids, grandkids, and a whole life.

Nibble clawed his way up onto the couch, a toy from Betty held tight in his mouth.

"You'd be living a pretty sad life here if it weren't for Betty." Carson said, trying to grab the toy from him.

Nibble swiped at his fingers with sharp little claws.

"We'll have to do something to thank her, won't we?"

He managed to snatch the toy from Nibble and threw it across the room. He grinned as the kitten scrambled after it.

Catching his reflection in the window, he paused to stare.

He was smiling. A real, relaxed, and joyful smile.

He slid off the couch to grab another toy. Nibble's little tail twitched in anticipation. He could slow down after this project was done. Look for a job that he actually enjoyed. Maybe he could keep Nibble.

Life with his neighbors and his kitten here could be good. Fulfilling even.

His phone buzzed. Dropping the toy, he picked up the phone.

He groaned and almost tossed it back on the couch. It was his boss. Again.

His finger hovered over the answer button. Did Tom really have to call on a Friday night?

Then again, he'd done it before. He accepted the call.

"Carson. I'm glad you're awake." His boss's brusque voice seemed to slice through his ear, and the weight that had been slowly lifting through the evening settled right back on his shoulders. "Something unexpected came up. Our clients have asked us to move the presentation to tomorrow morning. And of course I've told them that it's fine, but I wanted to make sure you've got everything ready."

Carson coughed. "Of-of course, but—"

"Excellent. I knew I could count on you. I know it's not ideal to come to work on a Saturday, but some of the team is planning to grab lunch together afterwards. So not a total loss, right?"

Carson nodded before realizing that nobody could see him except Nibble. He wondered if there was any point in telling Tom that he already had plans.

"Just make sure you're here bright and early," his boss said, "and nothing should go wrong. See you tomorrow."

Carson sank into the couch, staring at the phone.

Nibble attacked his arm.

Carson yelled, ripping his hand away from claws that seemed much too sharp for a kitten.

Nibble tried to paw at him, but Carson gently pushed him aside, wincing as the scratches began to bleed. "Sorry kitty," he muttered as he stood and went to the kitchen to wash the blood off.

He needed more coffee. He could *not* mess up this presentation, and he didn't have time for a kitten, or anything else for that matter.

Carson groaned, slapping his alarm clock. He grimaced at the stale taste of last night's coffee coating his tongue. Rubbing his eyes, he stumbled out of bed and wished today was over already.

In his dreams everything went wrong. First he was late, then his notes completely disappeared. He even lost his voice, ruining the presentation.

But that wasn't going to happen. Everything was going to go smoothly, his boss was going to be pleased, and he was going to get the promotion.

He hurriedly brushed his teeth and combed his hair, nearly bouncing at the thought of finally getting recognized.

He smiled as he came into the living room and said "good morning" to Nibble as he gathered all of his stuff.

His hand froze when he reached out for his laptop.

His work laptop. The one with all his notes. Containing everything he needed.

Covered in a stained mess of dried coffee.

"No, no, no," Carson muttered, his hand still hovering over his laptop. His ears rang, almost like the highway traffic had entered his living room. "No, no, no!"

He dropped to his knees beside the couch, and fumbled to open the laptop, his fingers sticking together.

He held the power button and waited. All deep breaths were met with the lingering odor of old coffee.

He continued pressing the power button, over and over again, until his finger ached.

But it was no use. The laptop was completely fried.

"Nibble, what did you do?" he yelled before burying his face in his hands.

He wanted to scream. And throw things.

How was he supposed to go into work now? How would he face his boss?

Nibble looked up at him and meowed as if insisting he was innocent. And also very hungry.

Except Carson couldn't see the little kitten he'd rescued from the parking lot. He only saw the face of a furry little criminal. The one who had ruined everything.

Betty had told him on that first night to put away anything he didn't want broken or ruined. She'd *told* him. And since he was terrible at listening, his presentation would fail. *He* would fail.

He stood and tried to breathe. There had to be something he could do.

His emails. He was always emailing his finished work to Tom, to his team. He could log onto a different computer and retrieve everything he needed.

Carson yelped as an insistent kitten started clawing up his leg, clearly unconcerned about any damage he might be causing. Pulling Nibble off his leg, Carson glared at him. He didn't have time to deal with Nibble, and he couldn't afford for him to break one more thing.

Still holding tight to Nibble, he pulled out the plastic carrier Betty had brought over. It was intended for vet visits and car rides, but it would also keep Nibble from getting into anything else important.

"It was just supposed to be for one night," Carson muttered. He sighed as he kneeled down by the carrier. He stuck his finger through the bars of the kitten jail as Nibble mewed rather pathetically. He tried to grab Carson's finger—without his claws this time—as if desperately trying to redeem himself.

"I don't know why I thought I had time for you," Carson whispered to Nibble, who obviously wasn't listening with his continued crying. "You probably would be better off at the shelter."

He stood, his skin prickling as the thought of the project came rushing back.

"I don't know why I'm talking to you. It doesn't matter." He grabbed his things and left without looking back.

Ten minutes until the presentation, with a borrowed laptop set up in front of him, Carson tried to push down the persisting nausea.

"Nervous?" Tom grinned at him, but it did nothing to set Carson at ease. He just nodded.

Tom nodded back. "Don't worry about it. Everyone gets nervous for their first big presentation." He frowned as Carson's phone rang. "You'd probably better turn that off before we start, though."

"Of course," Carson mumbled, nearly dropping his phone as he pulled it out of his pocket. It was Betty.

He answered and moved closer to the door, very aware of Tom's glare as he explained and apologized.

"It's no problem. We understand, dear. But it's still such a shame that they called you into work on a Saturday." Betty sighed before her tone switched to what sounded to him like forced chipperness. "I've been hearing Nibble crying all morning. I'd be happy to go and check on him if you'd like."

"No," Carson snapped, then sighed, pinching the bridge of his nose. Betty didn't deserve that. "I'm sorry, but he's fine. And even if he's unhappy, he'll be fine until I get back."

"Oh, all right." Even over the phone, Carson could hear her surprise. "If you're sure. You two were getting along so well, so I'm sure you know what's best."

"We were," Carson said, moving aside for some people to enter the conference room. They gave him a curious glance before settling down at the table and assembling their own papers and laptops.

"Were? Did something happen?" Betty asked before Tom called his name.

He flinched. "Coming!" The others were the clients. Obviously. "I'm sorry Betty, I've got to go."

He hung up before she could say goodbye and turned his phone on silent. It was time.

It was over. And it went *really* well.

Carson couldn't help but smile as he packed up his things.

His part of the project had gone especially well despite the borrowed laptop. The client had signed on right away, which was more than everyone had hoped for.

If that wasn't promotion material, Carson didn't know what was.

"Carson!" Tom swaggered up to him with a wide grin, and Carson grinned back. "That was fantastic! And I'm sure you'll do even better on the next one! I was thinking that you could stay here for a while and get ahead on some things for next week? Get ahead of the game."

Carson paused, a half-eaten cookie from this morning in his hand. "Oh, definitely." Even though he dreaded the idea. Then again...

"Sir, you mentioned a promotion awhile back? And since we did so well today, I thought we could talk about it sometime next week."

Tom laughed, but stopped a second later. "Oh, you're serious. Carson, you've only been here for six months! Surely you didn't think I meant so soon. That's not how the system works."

"Oh." His cheeks flamed. *Am I really that naive?*

Sure, he could do more presentations. He could keep working twelve hours a day if that's what the company needed. Get promoted eventually. That was what working a real-life job was like, right?

Something dripped onto the floor, so he looked down. The cookie was melting, slipping through his sticky fingers as his boss stared at him.

The cookies from his neighbors, from his friends. Was it possible to live in a world where life looked like more time with friends and cookies and kittens, and less time at the office? Could that be a *real* life?

"So, you'll be staying to work on the next presentation?" Tom called over his shoulder as he headed toward the door.

Gathering his courage and his briefcase, Carson slowly stood from the desk and wiped his sticky hand on a napkin. "I actually have an important appointment to keep this afternoon, sir. So I'm afraid I won't be able to today."

Tom raised his eyebrows. "Are you sure?"

"I'm sure."

Tom just nodded, his expression blank. "See you Monday then."

Carson waved and left the building as he often did.

Alone.

But it felt different now, like he'd woken up from a bad dream.

He sat in his car and grabbed his phone to look for the nearest open bakery.

"Okay." He muttered, starting the car. "They'd better have something with way too much chocolate."

Carson stood on the porch, Nibble in one hand and triple chocolate brownies in the other.

Since their car was in the driveway, Ed and Betty were home, but what if they didn't want to see him? What if this cancellation had been one time too many?

He knocked, bracing himself for cold words and a door slammed in his face.

Instead Betty greeted him with a tentative smile.

"I'm sorry about this morning," Carson blurted out before she could say anything. He took a deep breath and kept going. "And I was wondering, since I've missed so many dinners, if you'd like to have dessert?" He held up the container of brownies.

How could I ever expect anything but kindness from these people? he thought, as Betty's smile grew wider, and she ushered him inside.

"You're keeping Nibble?" Betty asked as they watched the cats play. They barely kept their swishing tails out of the roaring fireplace as they wrestled for a catnip mouse. Carson jumped to rescue Nibble from impending fiery doom, but the kitten leapt out of the way in the nick of time.

"Yeah, I'm pretty sure." He glanced sideways at Ed. "Not so sure I'll keep this job though."

Ed nodded, and though his expression was solemn, Carson could see the beginning of a smile. That was all the encouragement he needed.

"Well," Ed said, slowly pulling out his phone and typed in a number. "If you really want to look elsewhere, I've got a son looking for a computer guy for his business. I can put in a good word for you."

Carson grinned, watched his kitten, and listened to Betty go on about their son.

Maybe his life could look like this more often.

Carson set Nibble down on the couch before shoving the carrier into a closet.

He wouldn't be needing it for a while.

Dropping on his knees by the couch, Carson set his head on his arms and looked Nibble in the eye. "Sorry about this morning," he whispered. "Won't happen again."

Nibble purred, leapt off the couch, and scampered into another room.

Carson smiled.

His phone buzzed with a text from his mom asking how the presentation went, but more importantly, if they could come visit soon. He typed back a quick answer, "Absolutely."

This life was good.

LAUREN THOMAE

Ever since she was thirteen, Lauren Thomae has been babysitting foster kids, and now with an adopted sister of her own, she knows the importance of giving kids hope for their own happy endings. She writes Middle Grade fairy tales with those kids in mind, crafting stories that remind them to keep chasing the light. When she's not writing, she's trying to grow her hair to Rapunzel lengths, making hundreds of cookies, or convincing her siblings to read just one more story.

Achievements

- Completed two full-length novels and two novellas inside and outside of the Conservatory.

- Received professional developmental edits for both novels.

- Launched a House Cleaning business that earned over $8,000 in revenue in the first year.

- Has attended three writing conferences, including Write to Publish in 2023 and Realm Makers in 2024.

- Graduated from the Author Conservatory.

Pitches

- A *Rapunzel* inspired fairy tale where Rapunzel lives in a land that never stops raining. When her best friend (the prince) falls ill under mysterious circumstances she must brave the elements to find the antidote to save him, before it's too late.

- *A Pinch of Magic* meets *Tress of the Emerald Sea* in a Middle Grade Fantasy with sea snakes, light creatures, and a little sister who wants to grow up to be a brave lighthouse keeper just like her big sister.

- *Alice in Wonderland* meets *Encanto* in a Middle Grade fantasy with sentient magic closets and a younger sister grappling with watching her big brother grow up and preparing to leave for college.

BEFORE TODAY FADES

E.C. COLTON

Patterned scrapbook paper, printed photos, and bits of ephemera might look like they come nothing close to containing the magnitude of a life well lived, but I've always been up for a challenge.

The amber glow of the basement bulb seeps over the page as I fill the spaces between our family photos with cutouts. A string of family pictures—everyone wearing abnormally matching outfits and half-genuine smiles suspended in time—form an organic progression of Granddad's life as a grandfather across the page. They begin with him cradling my oldest cousin in the hospital and end with the last family photo we took with Grandma.

Now for the final page. I smooth a hand over the pulp of the cardstock paper. I've threaded photos of Grandma throughout the entire scrapbook, but I've always wanted to end this project with a spread committed to Grandma's seventy-fifth birthday party.

We didn't know it would be her last.

But it's one that never fails to bring a small smile to Granddad's face, and he'll need it as the fifth anniversary of her passing makes its slow approach.

I leave my office chair and navigate to the back end of the basement, stopping just short of cardboard moving boxes and a tangle of my family's possessions. I skim through the stacks in search of the only box that doesn't bear the usual Sharpied scrawl that marks it as full of my college belongings. The one that, instead, contains fragments of our family's bright but jumbled existence. I scoot a few across the carpet before my gaze lands on one in the corner.

The cardboard is shades darker than the others, shipping tape peeling away. As I lean down to pick it up, wet cardboard clings to my bare arm. I inhale mildew and gag.

And that's when my eyes land on the bloated wallpaper in the corner.

"Oh no."

My hand comes away damp, and I slowly take in the damage.

I encountered this at my dorm back in college—a scarring experience that left me and my roommate sleeping in facemasks all night. Nor did it help my sleeplessness after Grandma's passing.

It's a leak, probably due to poor insulation. And our family memorabilia might be ruined because of it.

"Mom, can you take a look at this really quick?"

Only a few seconds pass before I hear the thud of her slippers on the basement stairs. "What is it?"

I ease the box onto the worktable, inching it away from the scrapbook. "I think there's a leak."

She quickly assesses the damage, pulling boxes across the carpet, concern etching furrows in her brows. I can't tell if she's more worried about the memorabilia or the needed repairs.

I open the box, beads of moisture from it clinging to my hands.

The contents are a mess of uncategorized belongings. Soggy newspaper clippings from Granddad's time in the war intermingle with photos of my high school graduation extracted from photo frames. Rolls of developed film, now discolored, sit amongst a mess of dried flowers, candy wrappers, a vibrantly-printed package of seeds, and a few stray puzzle pieces.

I lift out one of the photo albums. Was it really over five years ago that I tucked photos from Grandma's party into the plastic sleeves?

Cracking the album open reveals pages of water-damaged Polaroids, blurred beyond recognition.

"Oh dear." Mom stands beside me, and I sink into the silence between us.

There has to be some way to salvage this final page. Preserve that last golden moment we spent together, to honor Grandma's memory and comfort Granddad when I won't be around.

"Try a blow dryer." Mom leans over, her head throwing shadows across the worktable. "Some of these might be salvageable."

"Maybe."

Mom squeezes my shoulder. "You could dry them upstairs. It looks like a leak in the insulation, I need to call the contractors before I run some errands with your granddad."

I load the photos into another cardboard box, then carry it up the stairs to my bedroom down the hallway, taking me through the living room.

The warm, muted scent of barley tea surrounds me, and I peer around the corner to find Granddad situated on the couch. His walker is within arm's length, and a mug of tea and his old Polaroid camera sits on the adjacent coffee table. He's smearing glue over a completed puzzle with a paintbrush that looks too large in his shaky hand. Today the scene weighs on me; a reminder that I'm leaving for a semester overseas tomorrow. I won't be home to support Granddad now, just like I was barely here after Grandma's passing.

Granddad looks up, and I force a smile. He may not know anything about the scrapbook, but he certainly won't know how badly things have gone awry.

"Almost done packing, Madison?"

The worry ebbs when I realize I look like I'm just gathering belongings from the basement.

If only it were that simple.

I force enthusiasm into my voice. "It's going well! Still trying to downsize from three suitcases."

"Got a moment?" Granddad gestures at the puzzle with his paintbrush, dotting glue across the coffee table. "You could help with the mounting. This would look real nice by the fireplace, don't you think?"

I'm tempted to forget the scrapbook momentarily, but I can't afford that luxury today. "I'm sorry, Granddad, I'm just a little occupied right now."

"Right, you've got packing to do." He returns to his puzzle.

I leave him to it, placing the box in my room before returning to the basement to retrieve the scrapbook, then the bathroom in search of a blow dryer. I plug it in and peel the Polaroids out of their sleeves. A few rays of afternoon sunlight seep through the latticed window, scattering cubes of light like checkers.

I skim the dryer over the photos. If I can squint hard enough, I can almost see outlines through the black splotches: The way the day was bathed in golden-hour sunlight that dissolved into a peach sunset; the hordes of people—relatives, family friends, Grandma's former coworkers—clustered around the bayfront lawn Mom reserved. I can almost see Grandma lighting up as the guests arrived, coming out of her normally reserved shell and even declaring she could bake a better pie than the ones my parents catered for the occasion.

We were all happy then. Floating on a rare kind of happiness you get from seeing those you love happy, too.

But that's just my memory breathing life into those photos, because it would take a miracle for anyone else to see them now.

I swap the dryer for rags, but to no avail.

I'm losing time.

"Is now a bad time?"

Mom stands in the doorway.

"Just a little bit." I hold up a Polaroid, and she steps over to take a closer look. "Even if I managed to dry them all, the water damage is pretty bad. You can't make anything out."

"Thanks for spotting the basement leak when you did. It's a big enough issue that the insulation contractor's on his way now to take a look."

At least something good came from this mess.

"The problem is, I need to be here when he arrives, but your granddad still needs to run his errands."

The realization hits me. Granddad's been relying more heavily on his walker recently. His arthritis must have worsened. "You need me to drive him."

"I know the timing can't get any worse, but it shouldn't take long." Mom brushes wisps of hair away from my head, and I lean into her warmth. If only I was still young enough to believe I could go to my mom with my problems, and she'd always miraculously make them right.

"Now that I think of it, he's planning on stopping at Edgar's store. He was at the birthday celebration. He might have some photos that you can use for the final page."

I release a slow breath. It might have to do.

If Edgar still has the photos, the final page isn't beyond saving. But if he doesn't, it'll be an afternoon wasted.

"Sounds good." I pull myself to my feet.

Mom gives me a worn smile before turning to go. "Thanks, Madison. That helps a lot. I'll go tell him."

I reach for my favorite coat, one of Grandma's old ones I've worn religiously as the semesters faded from one to the other. It occurs to me that perhaps I've always gravitated toward the weight of old things, the sacred sense surrounding them.

"Ready to go, Granddad?"

He gets up from the couch, reaching for his walker. He puts on a giant puffer jacket, the vintage Polaroid camera he carries everywhere already hanging around his neck. "Ready as ever."

I grab the keys to Mom's Honda Accord off the kitchen counter.

The end-of-summer air, quickly ripening into autumn, brushes past me as we head to the car. Once we're situated, I turn on the wipers to brush the fallen eucalyptus leaves off the windshield and pull out of the driveway.

"Mom said you wanted to stop by the puzzle store?" I ask.

Granddad nods. He's gone to the same one for as long as I can remember.

"Guess what? We're not browsing this time," Granddad says as we pick up speed. "This old man figured out the thingamabob to order online, so all I'll have to do is pick up my order."

His enthusiasm for such a small thing makes me smile. "How impressive."

Granddad sticks his camera out of the window, snapping photos of the California bay and me driving. The camera spits them out, and he shows them to me between stoplights, some blurred due to the car's movement.

I opt for the fastest route to town, and we soon pull into the familiar parking lot, usually stuffed with tourists' cars on the weekend, but today is mostly empty. I choose a parking spot close to the sidewalk, and as we leave the car, I take in the view. A stretch of sidewalk and storefronts stand silhouetted against the seafoam blue of the bay, framed by eucalyptus trees. It's Tuesday, so the streets have lapsed into silence, broken only by dishes clinking from the diner down the street.

A small cluster of people wander down the sidewalk. One of them—a lady with short, greying hair—lowers her sunglasses and studies in *Odds & Ends'* storefront, and I glance away as the glare of the sunlight against the parked cars hits my eyes.

This stranger lowers her sunglasses the same way Grandma did.

If there's a point where you stop seeing the person you lost around every turn, I haven't reached it yet. I'm unsure if I ever will.

But Granddad's still smiling, snapping a photo of the building with floorboards that practically creak with familiarity as we step through the doorway. Instantly, we're enveloped in redwood bookcases, stocked with puzzle and book displays. As I breathe in the scent of aged pages, I find my shoulders relaxing. There's a sense of peace that encompasses this place, as though it could solve the problems of anyone who steps through the door.

And in a way, if the photos are nestled somewhere in the back room, maybe it's true.

I make my way to the counter in the middle of the store, but Granddad—despite his arthritis—has already shuffled halfway around the counter and claps his old friend on the back.

"Good to see you, man." Edgar's bright, sunburned face matches the one in my memories. "And you brought Madison! Congratulations on graduating college. Where are you off to next?"

"I'm leaving for a semester abroad tomorrow, doing an animation internship with a studio in France."

My usual excitement for this opportunity has a dull tint. This time tomorrow, I'll be overseas.

How should I go about asking him for the photos without Granddad around?

Edgar whistles, supplying the enthusiasm I can't muster at the moment. "Impressive! Can't wait to see your work on the big screen one day." He glances back to Granddad. "That's got to be a big change, for sure. Could've sworn it was yesterday she was wandering around here, trying to replicate those drawings in picture books."

Granddad brightens. "No kidding."

I'm used to Granddad and his friends draining significance from the past. Any other day I'd be happy to slip into a comfortable silence as they reminisce, but today isn't one of them.

"That reminds me," I jump in, "we're here to pick up an order. I think it should be under Granddad's name?"

Edgar swipes at the monitor behind the counter before disappearing into the back room. "We should have it ready!" he calls over his shoulder. "Be right back."

Granddad watches after him. "Might take him multiple trips."

"How many puzzles did you order?"

"Your mother would say too many. Just five or six." Granddad rests his walker against the counter and takes a seat. He's got that glossy reminiscent look in his eyes again, as though he's rummaging through a file cabinet in his mind. "Your grandma would never say such a thing. She loved puzzles."

I curl my jacket sleeves over my palms at the mention of Grandma. When did Granddad's grief at her memory expand into something other than sadness? It seems as though his memories with her have metamorphosed into joy—not the last minutes we spent at her side after her cardiac arrest, with me resting my head on Granddad's shoulder.

My family has shared our grief over her death, cut it into tiny pieces and distributed it so we didn't have to bear it alone, but I've always felt I haven't done my part. I let supporting Granddad get tangled up in college deadlines that have left me with little time to be home. And now I won't be here to share it with Granddad.

That's what the scrapbook is for.

I check the time. It's twelve-thirty in the afternoon. If Edgar has the photos and we spend thirty minutes on Granddad's other errands, we should make it back in time to allow me an hour to finish.

But Granddad's talking, oblivious to my whole train of thought. "Well, at first she didn't see the use in them. All that effort for a photo when we could get one printed. But all that changed."

"That's nice," I say, but the ornate clock above the register pulls me into reality. I need to ask Edgar for help away from Granddad's earshot.

"She'd sit on the couch, reading, and I'd work on my puzzles. Sometimes she'd go 'no, that piece goes over there,' and be right every single time."

The minute hand on the clock inches over. Granddad keeps talking.

"She had an eye for puzzles, and I told her so, but she thought they were a waste of time. She'd much rather—"

Edgar cracks the door open, arms full of boxes. He places them on the counter and reaches for a large paper bag, stapling the order slip across the front. "This look about right?"

Granddad grins and leans over to pay. "Should be."

It's now or never. "Actually, I have a quick question about one of the items?" I continue through the redwood shelves as Edger follows, then lower my voice to a whisper. "Bit of an odd request, but do you have any photos from my grandmother's birthday party? I'm trying to put together a scrapbook page dedicated to the last good moments we had before her—" my voice snags on the word— "passing, and my original plan didn't quite work out. I need them by today because I'm leaving tomorrow."

Edgar's eyes brighten. "I do remember taking photos then! I'll see what I can find."

I exhale. "That would be perfect."

"Your secret's safe with me." He winks before returning to the counter and swiping at the monitor.

Granddad looks up from his walker, studying one of his puzzle boxes, the paper bag resting on his knees. "Ready to head out, Madison?"

"Edgar's just checking something for me. It shouldn't take long."

"I'm not sure we have an expansion pack like that, but I can check." Edgar's tone is casual, as if he's had countless conversations like this one before. "Give me a minute." He disappears through the rows of bookshelves, his footsteps echoing on the wooden staircase upstairs.

Granddad grins at me. "Ordering a card game? Sounds like something your grandma would do. Well, back before she loved puzzles."

There's no harm in talking to avoid looking suspicious. "She didn't like puzzles at first?"

Granddad sighs. "She said they would make her eyesight bad." He chuckles softly, his gaze moving past me. "Guess you weren't wrong about that."

Is he speaking to Grandma?

"When did everything change?" I ask.

"I'd leave out puzzles, and some days I'd catch her working on them." His expression folds into a faint smile. "She pretended it wasn't her, so I kept talking about how I was suddenly making such fast progress. But my big talk was too much. She confessed, and we'd work on puzzles for hours together. Come to think of it, it was her idea to hang them up on the walls of our first house."

I see Granddad again, the contented expression that crosses his face every so often as he regards his finished pieces and all the puzzles that line the walls of his room.

I should've known it all tied back to Grandma. In some small way, maybe this is his way of honoring her memory, letting those pieces of her live on through him.

Maybe he'd missed that today.

But the scrapbook.

Edgar appears again, his arms empty. His smile doesn't quite meet his eyes, and my hopes fray like denim.

"I couldn't get a hold of that card game, unfortunately." Edgar shakes his head. "Sorry about that, Madison. My daughter-in-law might've bought the last one, but I can give her a call and let you know."

"That would be great." It doesn't sound great, but a little hope is better than nothing. "I appreciate you checking, though."

"Well, you have a nice day!" Edgar's tone is decibels too chipper as he walks around the counter to hug us goodbye.

I smile, but it dissolves into the bay wind as we slowly head back into the parking lot. "Where to next, Granddad?"

"How about the fishing supplies shop?"

I turn on my phone's notifications on the off chance Edgar calls with news and back out of our parking space to head to the familiar fishing shop. *Bert's Marine Supplies* is perched on a wooden pier stretching into the bay, preceded by a string of pastel storefronts advertising bay sweatshirts and merch. Any other day I would've stopped to take in the view, enthralled by the waves crashing against the rocks below, but disappointment has drained the color from my world.

We parallel park across the street before Granddad tries the shop's door.

It's locked.

I peer through the window, shading my eyes against the sunlight's dull glare. I barely make out the darkened outline of tackle boxes and buckets lined up against the far wall.

"Looks like it'll be closed until the top of the hour." Granddad gestures at a makeshift "Out for Lunch" sign resting against the glass. "Let's get coffee while we wait."

I follow his gaze across the street, then at my phone, but no call notification. The day's quickly fading, but I need to stay in the area in case Edgar calls. "Sure."

Bells chime behind us as we enter the café, and in an instant, I'm enveloped by the clatter of mugs and the rhythmic whir of a coffee grinder. Unlike the cafés I grew accustomed to at college, this one is bathed in the glow from a large chandelier, with threads of sunlight seeping through the windows.

Granddad studies the wooden menu, and his eyes light up when he finds the "Create-Your-Own" option. "Want a surprise drink?"

I burrow my phone deeper into my pocket as though I could shutter the anxiety surrounding the scrapbook away with it. "Sure, sounds great."

The creases around his eyes make an appearance again. "Even better, how about we choose surprise drinks for each other?"

I nod and locate one of the kiosks, settling on a barley tea with strawberry syrup and a splash of oat milk, and Granddad slides his card over to pay. We find a table near the back, next to a speaker with lilting tunes that intermingle with the bustle of the café, and Granddad sinks into the seat of his walker.

I study the decor, the plants, and the clusters of customers before pulling my phone out again. I trust Edgar's doing his best to find the photos, but what if tracking them down is harder than anticipated? What if his daughter-in-law saw no significance in them and tossed them out?

The barista at the front calls Granddad's name, and I gather our drinks, placing the cups on our table.

"So what did you choose?"

I read out the label. "Barley tea with oat milk and strawberry. I thought you'd like it."

He takes a sip and contorts his face.

"Is it bad?"

"It tastes like one of your grandma's experiments." Granddad takes another sip. "That woman was adventurous in nothing except her tea."

I hesitantly try Granddad's order for me, an iced mocha with floral notes. "At least one of us has good taste."

Granddad chuckles. "After all those years of drinking your grandma's tea, you bet I do. She made tea every morning, and it would be different each time. She'd even mix up the tea bags so I couldn't tell what I was drinking."

I've never heard this story before, even after all these years of tasting Grandma's more questionable pastries. "What kind of combinations?"

"She'd mix syrups with tea that didn't need it. Sometimes she'd throw in lemon slices. Other times she'd add a dash of milk. Or even spices she'd find in the pantry, all mixed up." Granddad groans. "She'd up the sugar, too, if it tasted bad. I could tell, some days we drank straight sugar."

I picture Granddad sipping tea, faking appreciative nods, all while trying his best not to hurt Grandma's feelings, and I can't help but laugh.

He shakes his head in mock severity. "She couldn't make a normal-sized cup of tea. We'd be stuck with pitchers full for days."

"Why didn't you just tell her it was bad?"

"That'd be opening a whole new can of worms." Granddad tilts his head. "She'd go on about how tea shouldn't be wasted. And how a good morning always starts with good tea. What was I supposed to say, that the good part was debatable?"

Grandma was always so particular, but how much Granddad probably found himself in new situations because of it never before occurred to me. As I laugh, I can almost feel the knot of grief uncoil a fraction.

Maybe this is how Granddad allowed the loss to expand into healing. By choosing to remember, and share, the kinder moments over the ones sorrow claimed.

Choosing to remember her life, not just her death.

"That's quite the dilemma you found yourself in, Granddad," I say, trying to keep a straight face. "Did you ever end up telling her?"

"Of course not. When you love someone, sometimes you just grin and bear it. The good news is, I have a high tea tolerance now." Granddad takes another sip of his drink and winks at me. He then whispers in an undertone, "It's not so bad, don't worry."

The cuckoo clock on the wall chirps, announcing the top of the hour, and I swivel toward the exit as Granddad gathers his drink. "Ready to head out?"

He wheels his walker out, and before I join him, my gaze lands on our table in the corner, bathed in golden glow and shaded by shadows. When we leave, it'll inevitably fade into insignificance, seats filled with strangers.

If only there was something to tether me to that memory.

I pocket the receipt, and as I pass the counter to throw out our trash, my eyes find a stack of tiny business cards on the counter, the drink logo smiling up at me. I slide one into my jacket.

These may be mere fragments of the moment we shared, but they'll have to do.

Granddad is waiting outside, a worn pair of gloves on his hands. I've seen him hunched over them with a needle and thread, darning the holes now that Grandma isn't here to do it. There are a million tasks I wish I had the time to do, to help him out a bit, but I'm leaving tomorrow morning, and the day is quickly slipping through my fingers.

We cross the street to the fishing shop, the wooden deck creaking under my feet. He waves me toward the spot overlooking the bay and raises his camera.

"Smile, Madison."

I awkwardly fake laugh and lean against the railing as he presses the shutter, and the camera spits out another photo.

"Is that who I think it is?" Albert, another of Granddad's friends, emerges from the side of the building and plops two buckets down on the deck. He gives Granddad an enthusiastic hug, his knit red hat barely inching past Granddad's shoulder.

They exchange greetings, and Granddad gestures at the shop. "Was hoping to get a new fishing rod today."

"Fishing trip coming up?"

"No, staying local." Granddad chuckles. "Maybe I'll show Madison some tricks if the fish are still biting in a few months."

Likely his way of saying he misses me already.

"Come on in." Albert props the shop's door open with a brick and ushers us inside.

I inhale the fishy stench and take in the familiar scratched floors, the buckets lining the walls and shelves, and rods suspended from hooks on the ceiling.

Granddad maneuvers his walker inside and wastes no time trying on a fisherman's hat—an embroidered fish with "What's Biting?" across the front. "How's this look, Madison?"

"Stunning. Here, let me get a picture." I take the Polaroid from him and snap a photo, with Albert still in the frame. I pocket the photos, then hand the camera back to Granddad.

"So you're trying to get her into fishing?" Albert leans against the counter.

"That's the plan, maybe we'll look at some beginner things today."

Albert's eyes brighten. "Let's try some different rods, then."

He leads the way to the back of the shop, slowing down for Granddad, and he starts pointing out the different brands, pausing to test cast a few. I nod along to their lingo, barely understanding a word.

That's when my phone vibrates. I put down the rod Granddad handed to me and slide my phone out of my jacket pocket. My throat tightens, wingbeats of anxiety swarming my stomach, and it only increases when I realize it's Edgar's name lighting up the screen.

He could be calling because he's found the photos.

He could also be calling to inform me they're lost.

"I have to take this real quick." I hurry down the aisle and out onto the deck before picking up. "Hello? Edgar?"

"Madison! Glad I got a hold of you." I wince at the high volume and slide the phone a few inches away from my ear. "Good news, my daughter-in-law has a whole boxful of old photos, and found the ones I took at your grandma's party mixed in. She set them aside for you."

I lean against the railing, my legs suddenly shaky. "Oh, thank God."

"She lives two hours from town. She'll be home for the rest of the afternoon, so she's happy to have you pick them up if you can."

My phone lights up with a text. Edgar's just sent her address.

I dial it into my maps app, then glance at the time, trying to estimate how long it'll take. I could leave right now, get there by three, and make it back home by five, leaving barely enough time to pick up Granddad. I'd have to pull an all-nighter to finish the final page of the scrapbook with those photos, but it'd be worth it.

But that means Granddad will have to remain here for the next four hours. At the cost of getting the photos and finishing the scrapbook.

It should be an easy choice. I shouldn't be standing on the deck of the fishing shop, the tangle of dread returning. What if he's disappointed if I leave him here? What if he's disappointed I've cut our afternoon of sharing stories and snapping photographs and remembering Grandma short?

Footsteps shuffle on the deck behind me, so I turn. It's Granddad, pushing his walker.

"Oh, there you are! I wanted to show—" A mischievous grin brightens his face, but he quickly covers his mouth.

In an attempt to steady my thoughts, I turn toward the bay and trace the grain in the wooden railing with my eyes. Granddad being here doesn't make the decision any easier. He might be disappointed, but seeing the scrapbook and the comfort it brings him, he'll eventually understand the cost.

But his excitement gives me pause. The way his eyes lit up when he invited me to help him with the puzzle, the humor he found nestled in snapping photos while I was driving, and the peace that seemed to settle about him when he was reminiscing about Grandma.

Maybe all we were doing today was making little memories, ones that'll fade into insignificance someday, at least without some kind of reminder.

But this is the happiest I've seen him in months.

Maybe these memories matter more than I thought, despite how little we've had of them.

I swallow hard.

"Unfortunately, I'm going to have to pass this time, Edgar. Thank you for contacting your daughter-in-law for me."

"Totally understandable. Four hours both ways is a lot." Edgar grunts. "Enjoy the rest of your afternoon."

"Will do." I hang up, and despite the bay wind lashing at my hair, the shrill cries of seagulls, and the cacophony of waves below, a weight has been lifted from my shoulders, one I didn't even realize I was carrying.

The scrapbook will be okay. *I* will be okay.

Albert once again strolls around the side of the building with two lidded buckets and plunks them down on the deck beside me. "Ready to try some bait?"

Granddad grins. "Close your eyes, Madison, and reach inside."

"This better not be what I think it is." The last sight I see before inching my eyes closed is Granddad pulling out his camera. I reach into the nearest bucket and my hand touches something slimy that *moves*.

My eyes fly open. I've just reached into a bucket full of fat, writhing grubs.

Albert throws his head back, his booming laughter scattering a few seagulls from the dock. "Pull one out, Madison!"

I gently peel one away from the others and raise it high. The creature squirms before I set it down again, but Granddad's doubled over in laughter, leaning on his walker for support, only pausing long enough to hold up the Polaroid and snap a few photos.

"Second bucket! Second bucket!" Albert waves at me to close my eyes, and I oblige, resisting the urge to pull my hands out when they meet more liquid. I open my eyes and find a long worm coiled around my wrist. It leaves a trail of slime on my skin.

I don't know whether to join Granddad in laughter or choke in disgust.

Albert composes himself before calmly unwinding it and returning it to the bucket. "It's all bait. Got to get used to handling those before you start fishing. Rite of passage, so to speak."

"Give me three to five business years." I can't help laughing at Granddad, who's having a coughing fit, the Polaroid around his neck still spitting out a string of film.

After a few minutes, he calms down and Albert carries the buckets of squirming bait away.

"Don't you want to try fishing now, Madison?" Granddad teases.

"I think I'm good for now, thanks!"

We go back inside, and Granddad selects a new fishing rod. As we're checking out, I scour the wooden checkout rack for a grub sticker, similar to the one I had picked up, and add it to our purchases. Maybe I'll keep it on my water bottle as a reminder of home in a foreign country.

We say our goodbyes to Albert and head back to the car. There's a slight skip in Granddad's step as he maneuvers his walker and new rod into the passenger seat. Sitting comfortably, he starts riffling through his photos.

I take the meandering road back home, where Granddad snaps a few more photos of the bay. A strange sense of peace has settled over my bones, a sense that although the photos of Grandma's party aren't sitting in the backseat, the plethora of moments we've shared are worth the sacrifice.

If only there was a way to infuse the essence of those moments—the puzzle story nestled within the impatient silence of Edgar's store, picking each other's drinks at the café, and reaching into the buckets of bait at the fishing shop—into the final page.

We pause at a stoplight, and that's when it hits me. I can't help but mentally berate myself, because it's so obvious. The Polaroids scattered across Granddad's lap. The sticker, receipt and business card in my pocket.

All significant because of the memories we've made today.

It would be a perfect final page. A page that, while it doesn't contain photos of Grandma, celebrates the ways she lives on through us and through those moments.

The way we've made small steps to sharing memories of her with joy.

By the time I pull into the driveway, my hands are itching for the familiarity of scrapbook paper.

"Granddad, can I take a few of these?" I ask as I help him out of the passenger seat.

"Of course." He shoves the whole bundle into my hand.

Once he's settled in the living room, I rush upstairs. I select scrapbook paper in the same shade of warm gold that paints my memories—both of Grandma's party and the café where Granddad shared his story—and arrange the photos on top, annotating a few.

Finally, I paste a cutout of our drink receipt, the logo of the café we stopped at, filling the space with doodles of tea. As a final touch, I add the grub sticker.

The final page is nowhere near as perfect as I had imagined, but the mishmash of memories from today possess a certain beauty of their own. Tiny, almost imperceptible nods to the moments we shared.

Once the glue dries, I advance down the hallway.

I hold the scrapbook out, the floral embroidered cover Grandma would've loved. "I have something for you."

Granddad's again hunched over his puzzle. "You didn't take a grub home, did you?" But his face turns serious when he looks up.

I gently place the scrapbook on the couch next to him. "I know I haven't been home as much as I want to, and I won't be here for Grandma's passing anniversary, but I hope this honors her memory."

Granddad flips through the pages in his worn hands.

He reaches the final page, stares at it for a long moment, and pulls me into a hug.

"You like it?"

He taps the page, and his voice is soft, worn thin. "This one is perfect."

I relax into a smile. "I'm so glad we got to make memories today."

And somehow, I know there'll be plenty more to come.

E.C. COLTON

E. C. Colton grew up searching for comfort and encouragement within fictional worlds, reminders of hope on the other side of difficult situations. Now, as the author of the novella *Shards of Sky*, she writes contemporary and literary fiction stories about characters who mature and grow through their challenges, sometimes with a touch of magic. You can find her obsessing over all things blue food and cats, telling entertaining stories from everyday life, and chatting about personal growth over on her mailing list or Instagram.

Achievements

- Completed four novels, six novellas, and two short stories.

- Received two professional manuscript assessments on a novel and a novella.

- Gained marketing experience prior to joining the Conservatory by independent publishing a novella, *Shards of Sky*, in 2021.

- Has a mailing list of 200+ subscribers.

- Has experience consistently writing engaging emails and interacting with an audience through a mailing list for 4+ years.

- Completed in-depth marketing and business training through the Author Conservatory.

Pitches

- *Tomorrow, and Tomorrow, and Tomorrow* meets *My Friends* in an adult literary fiction novel about a stained glass artist vying for an opportunity to keep his artistic dreams alive.

- A YA historical fantasy about a girl cursed with a magical ability to manipulate gravitational fields who teams up with Albert Einstein to develop his theory of relativity—only she's not counting on being his long-lost daughter.

A NOTE FROM THE INSTRUCTOR

"In the beginning ..."
   "When I was a kid ..."
"Once upon a time ..."
Stories.

All of us have grown up surrounded by stories.

We read them, watch them, listen to them over the dinner table, share them when we come home from work and school.

Stories bridge the gap between cultures and generations. They bring together what has been and what could be.

Stories remind us of who we are and inspire us with who we can become.

In this volume, ten young writers used fantasy, science fiction, historical fiction, contemporary, and magical realism stories to bring us to another—often very different—time and place and show us there some very familiar people.

These are people who want to be brave but are afraid of the dark, who want to do great things but struggle with unforeseen obstacles, who desire family and don't know how to escape isolation.

If this collection of diligently crafted stories resonates with you today, it's because the writers first lived out the hopes, struggles, and triumphs in these pages.

They fought through personal fears and were brave. They risked stepping into community and were vulnerable. They strove to do big things and learn to, first of all, be faithful in the small ones.

Each story in this book is now two things: a glimpse of a fictional human, traveling a very real path, and a memorial to the real-life courage, diligence, and hard work of the story's creator. By holding this anthology, you are sharing in these young writers' lived stories. May the adventures here inspire you to look back and be encouraged—and to look ahead and dream.

Lauren Hildebrand
Head Fiction Instructor at the Author Conservatory

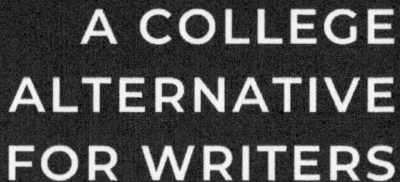

Made in the USA
Coppell, TX
15 December 2025